ENVIRONMENTAL SCIENCE
CHANGING POPULATIONS

Upper Saddle River,
New Jersey

CONTRIBUTING WRITERS	**CONTRIBUTORS**
Mary Jo Diem	*Zero Population Growth*
Janice Haymes	Deborah Brouse
Deborah Parks	Pamela Wasserman

REVIEWERS
Patricia Neidhardt
Robert Hubert

Cover Design: Richard Puder Design
Cover Photo: Image Finders/Dave Watters
Electronic Technical Art: Accurate Art, Inc.
Executive Editor: Joan Carrafiello
Project Editor: Doug Falk
Editorial Assistant: Keisha Carter
Production Manager: Penny Gibson
Manufacturing Supervisor: Della Smith
Senior Production Editor: Linda Greenberg
Production Editor: Alan Dalgleish
Electronic Interior Design and Production: Margarita Giammanco
Art Direction: Nancy Sharkey
Photo Researcher: Jenifer Hixson
Marketing: Sandra Hutchison

Photo acknowledgments appear on page 92.

ISBN: 0–835–90736–8

Printed in the United States of America
4 5 6 7 8 9 10 04 03 02 01

TABLE OF CONTENTS

CHANGING POPULATIONS

Case Study

Living at the Top of the World

In the summer of 1992, three dust-covered traders walked into Taklakot, a town in Tibet. The traders were Drokbas, or nomads from the central Tibetan plateau. They carried items for trade in saddlebags strapped on their goats. The items were blocks of salt, chunks of cheese made from yogurt, and twisted ropes made of sheep wool. They also carried bundles of cashmere, the soft wool that grows under the outer hair of goats.

The three Drokbas headed directly for the market. They spent the day bargaining with merchants from Katmandu, Nepal, and farmers from southern Tibet. The Drokbas collected no money; they traded their merchandise for goods. They accepted as payment bags of droo (barley), boxes of meeshery (unrefined sugar), and solid blocks of cha (tea). When they finished trading, the Drokbas led their goats on a journey back home to the Tibetan plateau. The journey took nearly two months.

Today there are about 500,000 Drokbas. They make up approximately 25 percent of Tibet's population. They live on a huge plateau, known as Chang Tang. Chang Tang lies north of the towering Himalaya Mountains. More than twice the size of Texas, Chang Tang is a land of stark beauty. It averages about 4,572 meters (15,000 feet) above sea level. But even higher land surrounds the area. The ring of snowcapped peaks keeps rains from reaching the Chang Tang plateau. Less

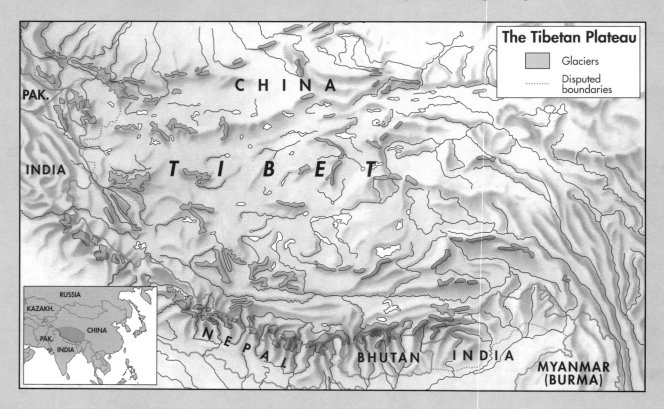

than 2.54 centimeters (1 inch) of rain falls there annually. Temperatures range from highs of 32°C (90°F) to 40°C (-40°F). The air is so clear that a Drokbas herder can be spotted up to 16 kilometer (10 miles) away.

In this awe-inspiring environment, the Drokbas thrive. For centuries, they have herded grazing animals on land that will not support farming. Yet, items that the Drokbas produce—especially cashmere—are an important part of Tibet's economy.

Few people outside Tibet have seen the world of the Drokbas. But Cynthia M. Beale and Melyvn C. Goldstein, two professors from Case Western Reserve University in Ohio, studied a community of Drokbas for more than a year. The Drokbas they studied lived in a 650-square kilometer (250-square mile) area known as Phala.

The nomads of Phala live along a salt-filled lake. They collect drinking water from freshwater springs in summer and from frozen chunks of ice in winter. Like other Drokbas, the nomads of Phala herd sheep, goats, and yaks 365 days a year. Yaks are a species of cattle adapted to high elevations and a cold climate. The Drokbas of Phala live at elevations of more than 16,000 feet, about the highest place to live of any people in the world.

The community of Phala consists of about 265 people. They live in some 57 households, organized into camps of two to ten tents each. The nomads of Phala live much like their ancestors, who moved into Chang Tang 8,000 to 9,000 years ago. The climate is harsh; they cannot farm. Even so, they consider the conditions of their lives a gift. In fact, they think their lives are much easier than those of the farmers on the southern edge of the plateau. One member of the community said to Beale and Goldstein, "Look: it is obvious that we have a very easy life. The grass grows by itself, the animals reproduce by themselves, they give milk and meat without our doing anything. So how can [anyone] say our way of life is hard?"

In 1950, armies from China invaded Tibet. In 1959, Chinese officials tried to force the nomads to keep their herds in certain pastures and to plant seeds for grass. They told the Drokbas that this was necessary to prevent overgrazing and to increase agricultural production. More than a decade later, the Chinese officials were embarrassed. They discovered that life on the plateau had gotten worse, not better. They quietly allowed the Drokbas to return to their own time-tested methods of living off the land. One leader of the Phala community explained:

We don't build canals to irrigate pastures, and we don't sow seeds to grow more grass. . . . [T]hat is not our way. The Chang Tang is a ferocious place. One minute the air is calm and the sun is shining; the next it is hailing. It isn't possible to alter the Chang Tang. We don't try; instead, we use our knowledge to adjust to it.

For the nomads of Phala, "adjusting" means moving people and herds from place to place. According to tradition, the Drokbas graze small herds of livestock in dozens of pastures. The pastures are spread over the community. No herd grazes in any one field for too long. In this way, the nomads have conserved their grasslands despite centuries of use.

As in the past, the nomads of Phala rely on products from the herds for food, clothing, and shelter. They make tents out of the hides of yaks. They weave clothes from the wool of sheep and goats. They make cheese, butter, and yogurt from the milk of female animals. But herding alone does not supply the nomads with all their needs. So the Drokbas trade livestock products for items unavailable on the plateau.

Goldstein and Beale's study shows that the population of Drokbas in Tibet is growing steadily. The number of births is higher than the number of deaths. The typical Phala household includes about nine people—two parents and seven children. This differs from the typical United States household, which averages 2.68 people. Surprisingly, the United States has a higher death rate than the nomads at Phala.

In recent years, the Chinese government has tried to control the number of children that Chinese people can have. However, they have not done this on the Chang Tang plateau. The plateau's huge land area still has few people compared to the rest of China. Tibet makes up 13 percent of China's land. But, as of 1990, only 0.2 percent of China's population lived there. For now, the Drokbas continue to prosper in their traditional ways.

1 POPULATIONS

These herders of Tibet, like herders elsewhere, keep a count of their domestic animal populations. These people depend on their livestock to make a living.

1.1 What Is Population?

In 1987, the Chinese government ordered the Drokbas of Tibet to reduce the size of their herds. The government insisted that the herds of yak, sheep, and goats were steadily increasing in size. The government said that these herds would soon overgraze and ruin the environment. The Drokbas of Phala disagreed. To find out if the number of animals in the herds was really increasing, the researchers Goldstein and Beale studied the domestic animal population of the Phala community.

A **population** is a group of organisms that breed with one another and live in the same space. This space can be a petri dish, a group of pastures, a mountain range, or an entire ocean. Members of a population belong to the same species. Examples are a population of amoebas in a petri dish, the population of yaks in the community of Phala, or the population of all the yaks in the world. You can study the population of the Drokbas or the population of all humans in the world.

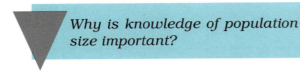

POPULATION SIZE

No population stays the same size indefinitely. Populations can change in size hourly, daily, seasonally, or yearly. Knowing how the size of a population changed in the past helps predict how it will change in the future.

In the case of the Drokbas, it was important to know the size of past herds that lived successfully on the Phala. This would help researchers decide if decreasing the size of the herds was really necessary.

The size of the population—plant, animal, or human—is extremely important. A population's size is often the key to its survival. An extremely small population can become **extinct** very easily. It can be wiped out totally by disease, a disaster such as flood, an increase in predators, or the destruction of its habitat by humans.

Inbreeding is common in small populations and can contribute to their extinction. Inbreeding is the mating of closely related individuals in a group of organisms. Continual inbreeding leads to genetic defects in the population, fewer offspring, and less ability to adapt to changes in the environment.

MEASURING POPULATIONS

Population size can be measured in two ways: counting and **estimation**. Researchers can count each individual of a population in an entire area. They can, instead, estimate the population by measuring sample groups.

A **census** is an example of counting. The goal of a census is to find and count every individual in an entire population. The United States government needs to know how large the U.S. population is; so it takes a census once every decade.

Sometimes, estimation is more appropriate than counting. Suppose you need to count the number of insect pests in an apple orchard of 100 acres. You want to turn loose ladybird beetles to eat the insects that damage the apple crop. You need a count of insects in order to decide how many ladybugs to let loose. But the insects are about to destroy the crop, and counting every insect will take months.

Instead, you could choose 50 trees at random in the orchard and just count the insect pests in each of these trees. This is called taking a sample of the population. Then you could find the average number of insects per tree and multiply by the total number of trees. This will give you a reasonable estimate of the size of the insect population in the apple orchard. It will take much less time than counting all the insects.

It is important to keep in mind that any measurement of a population is, in a sense, frozen in time. No population ever remains exactly the same size for long. A measurement of a population is only accurate in describing population size at the specific time that the individuals were counted.

The *number* of individuals in a population does not, by itself, determine the success of the population. Suppose there are two populations of guppies with 100 individuals in each. Both populations live in fish tanks with equal resources, such as oxygen and food, per liter of

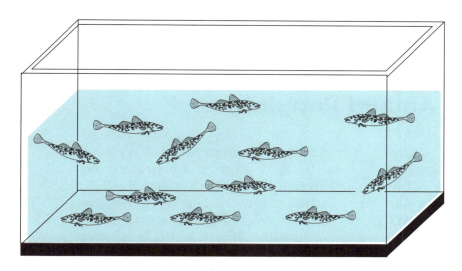
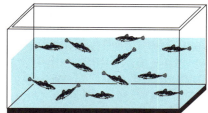

Two populations can be of equal size, yet differ in population density. Density is a measure of crowding.

water. But one population occupies a 50-liter tank, the other a 10-liter tank. The crowded tank clearly provides fewer resources for each guppy. The guppies in this tank have to compete with each other to obtain the food and oxygen. If there are not enough resources to go around, the guppies that are least able to compete may not reproduce.

You can see that the survival of a population depends more on the space for each individual than on the total number of individuals. For this reason, scientists often express the size of a population in terms of **density**. Population density is the number of individuals in a given amount of space.

SECTION REVIEW

1. What is a population? What is a census?
2. Give two reasons why a very small population is in danger of becoming extinct.
3. Why do you think the United States government takes a census? Why do you think the censustakers also ask the ages of the people whom they count?
4. To find population size for each of the following, indicate whether you would count individuals or whether you would estimate individuals: bacteria in a test tube, Tibetan antelopes in a herd, fireweed plants in Yellowstone National Park. Explain your choice in each case.
5. Why would knowing the density of the insects per tree for four separate groups of trees in your orchard be of more use to you than knowing the total number of insects in the whole orchard?

Lab Study

Measuring the Size of a Plant or Animal Population

All populations are not the same. Plant and animal populations vary in size and density, just as human populations do. Some wildlife populations are large and crowded; others are small and spread out.

Measuring the size of plant and animal populations can be a challenge. Some individuals are hard to count because they are hard to find. In some populations, individuals are so numerous it is hard to count them all.

In this activity, you will compare counting and estimating as methods of measurement.

Materials

    ruler
    work sheet
      Playground Populations

Procedure

1. Study the picture of the playground on the work sheet. How many different populations do you find? Record the name of each on the chart provided by your teacher.
2. Count the individuals in each population. Record this data on the chart in the row labeled "Actual Count."
3. Estimate the size of each population. Follow these steps:
   a. Use the row of numbers from 1-9 and the column of numbers from 0-9 around the playground to draw a grid of horizontal and vertical lines with a pencil.
   b. Select one of the boxes in the grid at random. Count the number of individuals of one population that you find within the box.
   c. Multiply the number by the total number of boxes in the grid.
   d. Record the total number in the row labeled "Estimate."
4. Repeat step 3 for each of the remaining populations in the box you selected.

Conclusions

1. Which population was easiest to count? Explain.
2. How did your actual counts compare with your estimated counts?
3. When estimating population size, is it possible to get a zero for a given population? If so, explain how.

For Discussion

1. When did the actual count method work best? When did the estimation method work best?
2. Why do you think researchers use the estimation method to establish the size of some populations?
3. Describe a situation in which neither method would be ideal for

POPULATION NAME	ACTUAL COUNT	ESTIMATE

establishing population size. Explain why.

Extension

Do research to find out about the "mark and recapture method" of estimating population size. Explain when this method would be good for establishing population size.

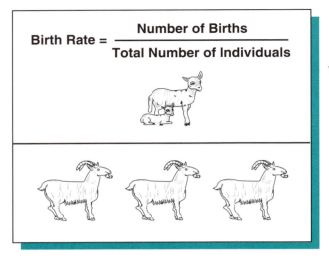

Birth Rate = Number of Births / Total Number of Individuals

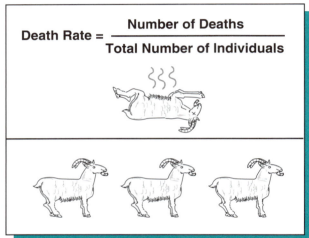

Death Rate = Number of Deaths / Total Number of Individuals

The number of births divided by population size gives the birth rate. The number of deaths divided by population size gives the death rate.

1.2 Growth and Decline of Populations

Professors Goldstein and Beale counted the number of sheep, yaks, and goats in the Drokbas' herds. They also kept close track of the number of births and deaths among the animals. They studied past census information about the herds. All this information

enabled them to determine if, and at what rate, the herds were growing.

How do scientists calculate the rate at which a population is growing or declining?

BIRTH RATE, DEATH RATE, AND GROWTH RATE

Researchers calculate the birth rate and death rate to determine how a population's size is increasing or decreasing. **Birth rate** is the number of births during a given time divided by population size. **Death rate** is the number of deaths during a given time divided by population size. Birth rate and death rate are expressed as numbers per unit of population per unit of time. In human populations, for example, birth and death rates are written as numbers per 1,000 people per year.

Population growth rate is the difference between the birth and death rates. It can be either positive or negative. Growth rate is often expressed as a percentage. This simply means the change in population per unit of time for every 100 individuals. To figure out the percent growth rate, the following steps are used:

- find the difference between number of births and deaths
- divide this difference by population size
- multiply by 100

When these calculations were made for the Drokbas' herds, the researchers found that the growth rate for the seven years between 1981 and 1988 was actually a decrease of about 8 percent. This would be written as -8 percent. A decrease of 4 percent (-4 percent) was due to natural births and deaths. Another decrease of 4 percent (-4 percent) came about because the Drokbas killed animals when the Chinese government told them to reduce their herds.

As you can see from the growth rate of the Drokbas' herds, when the size of a population decreases, it has a negative growth rate. You may be familiar with the term "zero population growth." This expression means that the birth rate equals the death rate. For example, if the birth rate is 6 and the death rate is 6, the growth rate is 6 minus 6, or 0.

▼ *How is growth rate affected by individuals who move in and out of populations?*

IMMIGRATION AND EMIGRATION

Emigration is the one-way movement of individuals away from a region. **Immigration** is the one-way movement of individuals into a region.

If there are enough resources and space in a region, individuals in a population usually stay there for their entire lives. Emigration occurs when the size of a population outgrows its resources. A population may outgrow its resources because it reproduces in great numbers. Sometimes, the resources in the region may decrease. This can happen if flooding or disease destroys the food supply. It can also happen as the result of slow environmental change that decreases the resources.

The region into which the individuals immigrate may already have a population of the same species living in it. The immigration will not be successful unless there are enough resources for both the old and new individuals.

To determine the total change in the size of a population, death and emigration rates must be subtracted from birth and immigration rates. For example, one million human deaths occurred in Ireland during the potato famine of the 1840s. Another three million people emigrated to other countries. The population of Ireland decreased by a total of four million individuals.

SECTION REVIEW

1. What are the definitions of *birth rate, death rate,* and *growth rate*?
2. If the birth rate of an animal population for a given time period is 7 births per 100 individuals, and the death rate is 8 deaths per 100 individuals, is the growth rate positive or negative?
3. The cattle population on a ranch is 2,560. In one year, 50 new calves are born and 100 cattle die. What is the population's birth rate, death rate, and growth rate?
4. Imagine a pond with two water lilies growing in it. The lilies' growth rate is such that each day the pond has twice as many lilies as it did the day before. It takes 30 days for the pond to be filled with lilies. On what day is the pond half filled with lilies? How many lilies fill the pond?
5. What are the definitions of *immigration* and *emigration*?
6. Why do you think the United States has a limit on immigration but none on emigration?
7. Imagine a population of animals in which some individuals emigrate when the population begins to outgrow the resources in its area. How do you think enclosing the population in a fenced preserve would affect it?

Field Study

Finding the Population Density of Organisms

To calculate population density, you establish the number of organisms in a specified population and divide by the area that the population lives in. The most commonly used units of area are square meters or square kilometers.

In this activity you will use the actual count or the estimation method to determine the population size of an organism in your schoolyard. Then you will calculate the population density of the organism.

Materials

meter sticks
string
stakes

Procedure

1. Your teacher will assign your team an organism that populates your schoolyard and will show you what the organism looks like.
2. Your teacher will help you identify the boundaries of the schoolyard and will tell you its area in square meters or square kilometers.
3. As a team, decide whether to use the actual count or the estimation method to establish the size of your population.
4. If you select the estimation method, then measure a square area in the schoolyard where organisms in your assigned population are found. Use stakes and

TEAM	ORGANISM	METHOD OF DETERMINATION	SIZE	POPULATION DENSITY
1				
2				
3				
4				
5				
6				
7				
8				

string to mark your square. Count organisms only within this marked area. Use this count to estimate the entire population in the schoolyard.

5. Determine the size of your population, and record it on the chart provided by your teacher.

6. Calculate the population density of your organism by dividing the population size by the area of your schoolyard.

Conclusions

1. Did you use the actual count or estimation method to determine the size of your population? Explain.

2. Describe the exact procedure you used to determine the size of your population.

3. Explain why it was easy or hard for you to determine the size of your population.

4. How reliable do you think your figures are? What factors affect their reliability?

For Discussion

1. Do you think the figures you obtained would be different if you repeated the measurements tonight? Tomorrow? Next year? Explain.

2. Study the class results. Do you see any relationship between the population density and physical features of the various organisms? Explain.

Extension

Repeat this activity at various times throughout the year. Compare the results and give possible reasons for any differences you observe.

1.3 Carrying Capacity of a Region

Professors Goldstein and Beale studied the way in which the Drokbas' graze their animals. They learned that the Drokbas graze their male yaks high in the mountains for nine months of the year. They take them from the pastures only when they need them for transportation.

The Drokbas graze their female yaks and their herds of sheep and goats in the pastures surrounding their base camp. They rotate these herds among several pastures. From September until early December, they graze the sheep and goats in pastures 10 to 40 miles away. From winter through spring, they move their female yaks higher on the mountain.

This rotation may seem like a complicated way to graze animals. However, the Drokbas are trying to make the best use of their limited resources without using them up. The herds eat the new-growing grass at the home base during the summer. In the fall and early spring, they move on and eat from different ungrazed pastures. The long months of good grazing provide the animals a thick store of fat and fur to last through the winter. In late winter and spring, the herds graze on what is left of the pastures at the base camp.

The Drokbas rotate the herds through different pastures in the summer. This gives the grass several days at a time to regrow.

The Drokbas understand that each of the pastures can support only a certain number of animals for a limited amount of time. They recognize the carrying capacity of their land for grazing. The **carrying capacity** of a region is the number of individuals of a species that the region can support at one time. The amount of resources in a region determines the region's carrying capacity.

How do changes in the carrying capacity affect a population?

CHANGES IN CARRYING CAPACITY

A region's carrying capacity for a population is not always the same. Carrying capacity often changes with the seasons, for example. This is the case on the Tibetan plateau. Changes in carrying capacity also occur when a change in the environment reduces or increases a region's resources.

A change in carrying capacity can affect a population's size. If the carrying capacity decreases below a level that meets the needs of the population, some individuals will die. However, if the size of the population increases beyond what the carrying capacity can support, individuals will die. In both cases, individuals will continue to die until the size of the population is again at or below carrying capacity.

Sometimes, a population that is growing rapidly exceeds its carrying capacity. One outcome may be that part of the population emigrates to another area. Another outcome may be a population crash. A population crash is a rapid and massive decrease in population due to death. If the population drops below a minimum size, the population may not survive and could become extinct.

The black-footed ferret of the United States is an example of a population that dropped below the survival level. Black-footed ferrets mainly eat prairie dogs. The ferrets take over and live in the prairie dogs' burrows. Ferrets used to be found in the grasslands from Texas to Canada. But farmers conducted a mass extermination campaign against the prairie dogs in the 1950s. Because prairie dogs were the main food supply of ferrets, the black-footed ferrets became extinct by 1960, or so people thought. In 1981, a population of 100 ferrets was discovered in Meeteetse, Wyoming.

The small ferret population was not safe, however. In 1984, another population crash occurred. Disease killed roughly half the population. Captive-breeding programs have been going on since the rediscovery of the ferrets. Only time will tell if enough population growth occurs to keep the animals from extinction.

What in the environment limits the size of a population?

LIMITS TO POPULATION GROWTH

The environment consists of both living and nonliving elements. The living elements include all the plant and animal populations. The nonliving elements of the environment include such things as water, soil, and amount of sunlight. In any region, the living and nonliving elements together make up and interact in what is known as an ecosystem.

Under ideal conditions, a population in an ecosystem increases at its maximum growth rate. But in every ecosystem, certain factors limit population size. These are called **limiting factors**. There are two kinds of limiting factors. **Biotic** limiting factors refer to the activities of the living things in the ecosystem. **Abiotic** limiting factors refer to the nonliving parts of an ecosystem. Both biotic and abiotic limiting factors combine to determine the carrying capacity of an ecosystem.

A population of predators, such as the black-footed ferret, must have a sufficient population of prey in order to survive.

Biotic limiting factors A number of biotic limiting factors regulate population size. These factors include:

- availability of food
- rate at which individuals in the population reproduce
- the number of predators in the ecosystem
- the ability of individuals to avoid predators
- emigration
- the ability of individuals to resist disease
- competition from other species and among individuals of the same species

As an example, consider the inability to resist disease. How does this limit the population? The Irish potato

Population size in large animals, such as this caribou, is limited by weather, food availability, and other environmental factors.

population was unable to resist a certain fungal disease. The disease spread through the population of Irish potatoes and wiped it out.

The biotic limiting factor that most often regulates the size of a population is availability of food. The amount of food in any one ecosystem is limited. Therefore, the size of the population that the ecosystem can feed is also limited. If there is not enough food for a population, individuals will starve to death. The lack of prairie dogs as a food source nearly wiped out the black-footed ferret population.

In most populations, some individuals are better able than others to compete for resources. The individuals that are least able to compete will die.

Many of the biotic limiting factors are closely linked to population density. As the population approaches and exceeds carrying capacity, limiting factors more and more reduce the popula-

tion. In other words, death rate increases with overcrowding. Biotic limiting factors reduce the population until it is again below the carrying capacity.

How do biotic limiting factors act on an overcrowded population? Overcrowding may increase competition among individuals of a population. Overcrowding may make hiding from predators more difficult. Diseases travel more easily between closely spaced individuals. For example, a contagious viral disease killed a number of black-footed ferrets that were in a captive-breeding program in Wyoming.

Abiotic limiting factors   Abiotic limiting factors include:

- climate
- amount of daily sunlight
- amount of rainfall
- temperature
- pollution by humans
- the nutrients in soil or water

Animal populations tend to be more limited by biotic than abiotic factors. Populations of plants, on the other hand, tend to be more limited by abiotic factors. For example, the plant density of the Drokbas' pastures depended on the amount of moisture in the soil and the consistency of the soil.

Abiotic factors can have an effect on some animal populations. Temperature and amount of water affect the size of the mosquito population in the northern United States. Summer rains leave pools of water in which mosquitos breed. Mosquitos also need warm temperatures to survive. After the first heavy autumn frost, most of the mosquitos in the northern United States die.

Another abiotic factor that affects animal populations is the amount of nutrients in the water. For example, fertilizers applied to lawns or farms sometimes cause pollution in lakes. These fertilizers greatly increase the nutrients in the water. Nutrient-rich water quickly speeds the growth of the algae population. This, in turn, means that an increase in algae deaths soon occurs. Bacteria, which decompose the dead algae, then grow in population. The increase in bacterial decay can use up most of the dissolved oxygen in the water. Many of the fish suffocate as a result.

HUMANS AND LIMITING FACTORS

Scientists are in disagreement about whether the human population has an upper limit. Is it possible for humans to reach their carrying capacity on earth? Some scientists believe they cannot. They think that technological advances in food production and disease control will keep up with human population growth. Other scientists feel that at some point, the earth will no longer be able to provide enough food for everyone. Scientists are also concerned about the effects of unlimited human population growth on the survival of many of the other species that share the earth.

Why is clumping the most common pattern of population distribution?

POPULATION AND DISTRIBUTION OF RESOURCES

Distribution is the pattern in which a population is spread out in the space it occupies. The location of resources in an ecosystem affects the distribution of populations.

Some populations, mostly of plants, have a **random distribution**. This means that the individuals are spaced irregularly throughout an area. Other populations, mostly of invertebrates, have a **uniform distribution**. This means there is an equal distance between each individual.

But the most common pattern of distribution is clumping. With clumping, separate groups of individuals are scattered throughout an area.

Clumping is the most common distribution pattern because most resources are not distributed evenly. They are distributed unevenly throughout an ecosystem and throughout the world. For example, some trees have more leaves than others. In an area filled with trees, more caterpillars will be found in the trees with the most leaves.

The human population is also distributed in clumps. Areas along rivers and near bodies of fresh water have a higher carrying capacity for humans than arid regions do. Water is an essential resource for humans. It also provides a quick means of transporting resources to the population. Therefore, human societies tended to develop around bodies of water. Few human societies have occupied deserts.

Because of modern transportation and technology, humans are not as limited by the distribution of resources as they once were. If one country has a resource needed by another, the two countries may work out a trade. Sometimes, however, countries benefit by having most of a resource needed by other countries. Middle Eastern countries, for example, have most of the oil that other countries need for energy.

Some countries, such as the United States, have a great deal of useful farmland. The United States is able to produce enough grain to feed its own population and to export to other countries, such as Somalia. Somalia is experiencing severe drought. Somalia's dry farmlands cannot produce enough grain to feed its population. Many individuals have died there of starvation. Other countries have provided food and technology to help feed the people of Somalia. Unfortunately, political problems in Somalia have prevented much of the food from reaching the individuals who need it.

You Solve It

A census can provide information about the size, composition, and distribution of a population. The information can be used in many different ways. Throughout history, governments have used census information to measure military strength and to set taxes. The United States Constitution mandates that a federal census be taken every ten years.

Governments are not the only agencies that take censuses. Your school district also takes a census of the population that it serves. Find out about your school district's census.

Find out when and how often your school district takes its census. How is the census carried out? What type of questions are asked on the census form?

Invite the superintendent of your school district to visit your class. Have the superintendent explain how the census information is used to plan for future needs of the school district.

Obtain the census results for your school district for the last six years. Compare the data of each census.

SECTION REVIEW

1. Why do the Drokbas rotate their herds though several pastures during the year?
2. What are limiting factors? Which biotic limiting factor is the major regulator of the size of an animal population?
3. Why wouldn't temperature be much of a limiting factor on the mosquito population in Florida?
4. What is carrying capacity?
5. How can a herd of grazing animals, such as sheep, change its ecosystem in a way that changes the ecosystem's carrying capacity?
6. Why is it important to know the distribution pattern of a population when estimating its density?
7. How has modern technology decreased the need for humans to live near freshwater supplies?
8. Why would researchers study the distribution of prairie dogs in a national park before releasing black-footed ferrets there?

FOR DISCUSSION

1. What changes do you see in the data from one census year to the next?
2. What trends do you observe?
3. How might these changes or trends affect your school district?

2 HUMAN POPULATION GROWTH

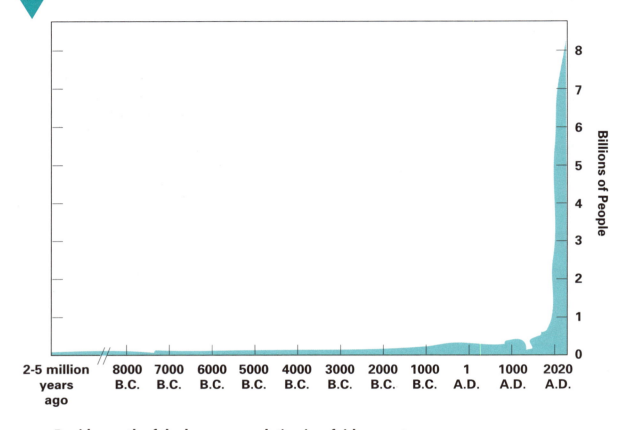

Rapid growth of the human population is a fairly recent process.

Humans are extremely intelligent. They have been able to populate every part of the globe that can possibly be lived on. They've overcome the limiting factors (predators, climate, disease, food shortages) that keep animal populations in check. The human population has grown to exceed the carrying capacity of many world regions. Overpopulation now strains the earth's life-support systems. Some people argue that overpopulation is one of the leading environmental problems of our time.

2.1 The History of Human Population Growth

For most of human history, the population grew very slowly. People lived on earth for about three million years with roughly the same population. Birth rates and death rates were in balance. Although birth rates were high, death rates—particularly among children—were also high. This was due to famine, war, and disease.

In approximately the year 1600, the population of humans reached 500 million. By the end of the 1600s, however, the balance of birth and death rates began to change. In Europe, the discoveries of the Industrial Revolution helped people to live longer. Advances in medical technology and public health dramatically lowered death rates.

Before the Industrial Revolution, not much was known about germs and how to fight infection. Water was impure. Wastes were disposed of improperly. People's cleanliness was poor. There were many insects and rodents. As a result, deadly diseases such as cholera, malaria, and typhoid spread easily. During the 14th century, for example, the bubonic plague, spread by rats, killed 75 million people in Europe. That was one-third of the population!

In the late 17th century, the microscope was invented. Scientists began to observe tiny life forms such as bacteria. They realized that bacteria cause diseases. With this knowledge, scientists were able to develop cures for specific diseases. They also understood the importance of cleanliness in preventing the spread of harmful bacteria.

In recent decades, the discovery of antibiotics and vaccines has eliminated some deadly diseases. Modern water- and waste-treatment facilities have lessened the risk of infection.

The Industrial Revolution has also led to improvements in diet. Modern farm machinery enabled farmers to produce more food in greater varieties. Railroads transported this food to millions of people over thousands of miles. Refrigeration kept the food fresh during transportation and after it was in people's homes. Nutrition and overall health improved.

As a result of these improvements, **life expectancy**, or the average number of years people live, increased. Death rates fell, birth rates remained high, and the population grew steadily. The Industrial Revolution in North America and Europe was at its height in 1800. At that time, world population reached one billion.

In 1978, Thomas Malthus, a famous English economist, wrote *An Essay on the Principles of Populations*. He warned that human population growth would overtake the food supply. He predicted mass famine and misery. He said something had to be done to slow growth.

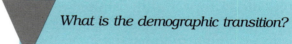

What is the demographic transition?

THE SHIFT OF POPULATIONS TO THE CITIES

The invention of modern farm machinery during the Industrial Revolution changed peoples lives. Less people were needed to produce food. Throughout Europe and North America, many people left farms for homes and jobs in the cities. The cities began growing in size. Without land to farm, large families became unnecessary and impractical. Children were more of an expense than a help in expensive urban areas. Slowly, birth rates decreased in nations that were industrializing rapidly.

The population pattern that took place is referred to now as the **demographic transition**. The demographic transition consists of three stages. There is an initial period of high birth rates and high death rates. This is followed by a stage of high birth rates and low death rates. Finally, there is a period of low birth and death rates.

Over the past 300 years, the populations of North America and Europe have gone through the demographic transition. Before the Industrial Revolution, they had high birth and high death rates. After industrialization, with its scientific and medical advances, death rates decreased while birth rates remained high. With economic growth and widespread access to education, birth rates came down to match the lower death rates.

The industrialized countries that have gone through the demographic transition are known as developed countries. Generally, these are countries in the Northern Hemisphere. They include Europe and the United States.

While the developed countries were going through this demographic transition, countries in the Southern Hemisphere were still experiencing high birth and high death rates. These includ-ed countries in Latin America, Africa, and Asia. These countries have still not completed the demographic transition. They are known today as developing countries. Mexico is one of them.

By the middle of the 20th century, the medical advances of the developed countries had spread around the world. Death rates in developing countries began to drop dramatically. But the population of the developing countries was still largely rural. They required large families to work the land. Birth rates remained high.

Unfortunately, economic conditions in the developing countries didn't improve as life spans increased. With high birth rates and low death rates, the populations were growing rapidly. By 1960, the world population reached three billion. Just 15 years later, in 1975, the population soared to four billion. In 1987, it topped five billion!

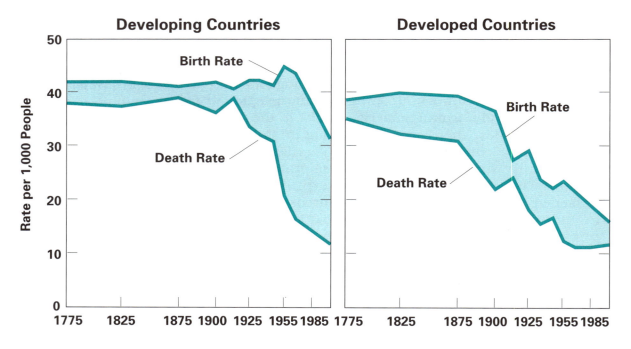

The growth rate of a population is the difference between the birth rate and death rate. If either the birth or death rate changes, growth rate changes.

Most of the population growth after the year 2000 will take place on the continents of Africa and Asia.

By the year 2000, the earth will probably have more than six billion people. Much of the developing world is still caught in the middle of the demographic transition. The rapid population growth has created widespread poverty.

SECTION REVIEW

1. What factors have contributed to the world's "population explosion"?
2. What is the demographic transition?
3. At what stage of the demographic transition are the developing countries?
4. How has the role of children changed throughout history in industrialized countries?

FOR DISCUSSION

How do you think Thomas Malthus's theory on population would be judged today?

Lab Study

Lots of Lemna

The human population has had an exponential growth pattern over the past 300 years. This means that the population has been doubling at an ever-faster rate. To better understand an exponential growth pattern, you can observe the growth of Lemna (duckweed) plants.

As individual Lemna leaves grow and enlarge, they break apart from the parent plant and form new plants. Before long, the new Lemna form a population of floating plants on the surface of the water.

Materials

10 Lemna plants (duckweed)
10-gallon aquarium with aged water and single-pump aerator

Note: *Leave the aquarium light on throughout the lab activity. Replace water when it begins to evaporate.*

Procedure

1. Work with a partner. Estimate and record the number of days, weeks, or months that you think it will take for
   a. the Lemna to reproduce
   b. the population of Lemna to double
2. Construct a data table in your notebook with columns for "Date" and for "Population Size of."

3. Every other day, take a few minutes to count and record the number of Lemna in the aquarium. Continue for five to six months or until the surface of the aquarium is completely covered. When the plants are too numerous to count, devise a method for estimating the percentage of the surface covered by the Lemna. Then estimate the population as follows.
   a. Calculate the surface area of the aquarium in square centimeters.
   b. Average, from ten samples, the number of Lemna plants per square centimeter.
   c. Estimate the percentage of the surface covered by the plants.
   d. Estimate the population by multiplying the numbers you obtained in a, b, and c.
4. When the Lemna cover the surface and you have finished collecting the data, make a graph of population size versus time, using the data from your table.

Conclusion

What is the shape of your graph? What do you think this means?

For Discussion

1. If organisms follow an exponential growth curve such as the one you graphed, why isn't the world hope-

POPULATION SIZE OF LEMNA		
DATE	POPULATION SIZE	POPULATION CHANGE SINCE LAST COUNT

lessly overpopulated with plants and animals?

2. What are some factors that might limit the growth of the Lemna population in nature?

3. Why has the human population followed the J-curve?

Adapted by permission from the National Association of Biology Teachers. The original activity, "Using Lemna to Study Geometric Population Growth, The American Biology Teacher" by Larry DeBuhr, appears in vol. 53, no. 4, April 1991, pp. 229-232.

2.2 Human Populations Today

In the time it takes you to blink, three people are added to the world's population. Every day, the population increases by 250,000; every year, by 93 million. This is the equivalent of adding the population of Mexico to the world annually. Most of the population growth—about 94 percent—occurs in the developing countries. Presently, three-fourths of the world's people live in the developing countries. With the exception of a few countries, birth rates are higher than death rates throughout the world. The world's population is continuing to grow.

What is "the rule of 70"?

POPULATION'S RAPID GROWTH

Over the past 300 years, the world's population has been growing at an ever-faster rate. For example, world population doubled from 500 million to one billion between 1600 and 1800 (200 years). It doubled from one billion to two billion between 1800 and 1930 (130 years). It doubled from two billion to four billion between 1930 and 1975 (45 years).

Population grows quickly even when the growth rate remains the same. Consider a country with a population of 100,000,000 and a growth rate of 2 percent. Its population will increase by 2,000,000 the first year (.02 x 100,000,000). It will then have 102,000,000 people. In the second year, the population will increase by 2,040,000 (.02 x 102,000,000). The total number of people will then be 104,040,000 people. In the third year, 2,080,800 (.02 x 104,040,000) will be added to the population for a total of 106,120,800 people, and so on.

In 1993, the world's population reached 5.5 billion. The growth rate was 1.7 percent. This may seem like a small rate of increase, but it isn't. It translates into large numbers of people added to the population each year. A 1.7 percent increase added 93 million people to the world's total in 1993. If this growth rate continues, the world's population will double in just 40 years.

Doubling Time   If you know the annual growth rate, you can predict the doubling time of a population. **Demographers**, scientists who study human population trends, apply "the rule of 70." The rule of 70 is very simple. When the growth rate remains the same, you divide the growth rate into the number 70 to find the doubling time of a population in years. A population growing steadily at the rate of 1 percent would double its population in 70 years (70 ÷ 1 = 70).

Kenya has a rapidly growing population. Its growth rate in 1993 was 3.7 percent. Its population will double in just 19 years (70 ÷ 3.7 = 19). On the other hand, Japan has a slow-growing population. The growth rate is 0.3 percent. Japan will not double its population size for 217 years (70 ÷ 0.3 = 217).

Population growth rates rarely stay the same for long periods of time, however. For that reason, the rule of 70 is not truly a method of predicting future populations. It is useful for describing what would happen if growth rates stayed the same.

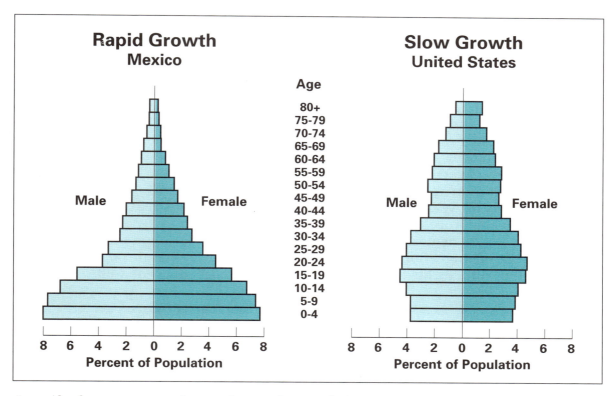

	Age	
Rapid Growth Mexico	80+ 75-79 70-74 65-69 60-64 55-59 50-54 45-49 40-44 35-39 30-34 25-29 20-24 15-19 10-14 5-9 0-4	**Slow Growth** United States

A graph of age structure gives a picture of a population. A pyramid shape with a wide base means that young people make up a large segment of the population.

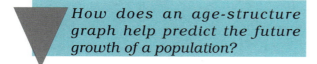

How does an age-structure graph help predict the future growth of a population?

POPULATION AGE STRUCTURES

Much can be learned about a country's population patterns by studying its **population age structure**. Demographers make age structure graphs like the ones shown on this page. One side of the graph shows the percentage of males in each age category. The other side shows the percentage of females in each age category. Demographers use the age-structure graphs to show population trends and to help make predictions. These graphs differ for fast- and slow-growing populations.

Kenya and India are examples of countries experiencing rapid population growth. In these countries, one-third to one-half of the population is under the age of 15. Older age groups represent much smaller portions of the total population. The age-structure graphs for these countries resemble triangles or pyramids. These countries can expect continued population growth as the people under age 15 enter their childbearing years. Most developing countries fit this pattern.

The United States is an example of a country with a slow rate of growth. The U.S. population is more evenly distributed among all age groups. Several countries in Europe have reached zero population growth (ZPG). Their populations are stable (unchanging) because births plus immigration equal deaths plus emigration. The age-structure graphs for these countries resemble rectangles.

In a few countries, high life expectancy and low fertility rates result in populations with more senior citizens than young children. The age-structure graphs for these countries resemble an inverted pyramid.

Today, the average life span is between 70 and 80 years. Therefore, a country's age-structure graph depicts 70 to 80 years of its demographic history. The effect of migration, war, and famine on the country's birth and death rates can usually be observed in the shape of the graph. The "baby boom," for example, can be seen in the graph.

The baby boom refers to a period of prosperity after World War II. During this time, many couples chose to have more children. Today, the "baby boomers," born between 1946 and 1964, make up the largest segment of the U.S. population. The bulge can be seen in the U.S. age-structure graph. Conversely, the Great Depression in the 1930s discouraged most couples from having more than one or two children. The decrease in population can be seen in the graph as well.

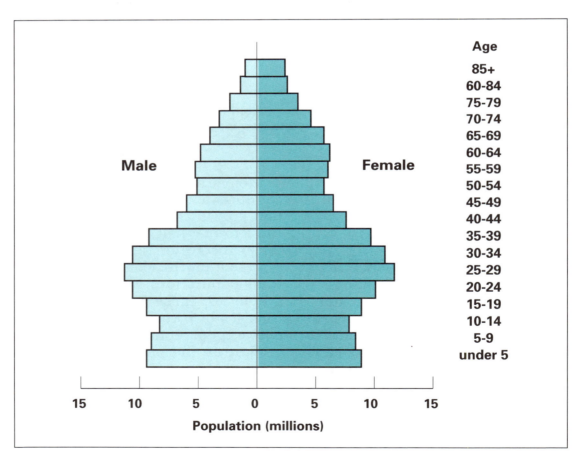

The United States population contains a smaller proportion of children compared to most other nations.

POPULATION GROWTH IN DIFFERENT REGIONS

Most regions of the world are experiencing population growth. The populations that are growing most rapidly, however, are in the developing countries of Africa, Asia, and Latin America. In these countries, the birth rates are significantly higher than the death rates. The annual growth rates range from 1 to 5 percent.

Developing countries usually have higher total fertility rates than developed countries. The total fertility rate is the average number of children that a woman has during her reproductive years (15-49 years old).

For the number of humans to stop increasing, the population must achieve replacement-level fertility throughout the world. Replacement-level fertility is an average of two children per couple. Even after a population achieves replacement-level fertility, the population may continue to grow for another 50 to 60 years. Growth will continue if a large segment of the population is in, or approaching, childbearing years.

There are a number of reasons why couples in developing countries have more children than those in developed nations. Two-thirds of people in developing countries live in rural areas. Parents in these areas depend on their children to help grow food and gather water and wood for fuel. Parents also depend on their children to care for them in old age.

In addition, the **infant mortality rate** is generally higher in developing countries. The infant mortality rate is the number of infants (per 1,000 born) who die before their first birthday. Where the infant mortality rate is high, couples tend to have more children. They want to be sure some of them live to adulthood.

The role of women in the society also affects fertility rates. In many developing countries, women lack opportunities for education and work. In these countries, women are respected primarily for their ability to raise children and farm the land. So women tend to marry young and begin having children while still teenagers.

In many instances, couples in developing nations wish to limit their family size but can't. They don't have access to family-planning information and contraceptives. According to the United Nations, women in Latin America, Asia, and Africa would have one-third fewer births if they could limit them to the number they wanted.

POPULATION DISTRIBUTION

Population distribution and growth rates vary from one region of the world to another. The following descriptions of the population patterns of each world region are based on 1993 data.

Developing Nations Asia has 20 percent of the world's land area. It is home to over 60 percent (three-fifths) of the world's people. In fact, the greatest concentration of people on earth is in China. China has 21 percent of the world's population—over one billion residents! The Chinese government has become aware that China's natural resources can't sustain such a large population. As a

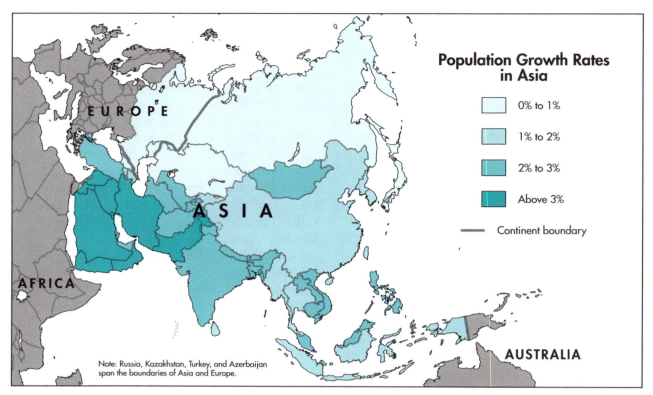

Population Growth Rates in Asia

- 0% to 1%
- 1% to 2%
- 2% to 3%
- Above 3%
- —— Continent boundary

Note: Russia, Kazakhstan, Turkey, and Azerbaijan span the boundaries of Asia and Europe.

EUROPE

ASIA

AFRICA

AUSTRALIA

The nations of southwest Asia have the highest population growth rates on the continent.

means of curbing growth, China has enforced a policy of one child per family for the past 20 years (See Chapter 3).

India, the world's second most heavily populated country, has 16 percent of the world's population. It is home to nearly 900 million people. Another 8 percent of the world's people live in the islands of Southeast Asia, including Indonesia, Thailand, and the Philippines. Overall, Asia's growth rate is 1.7 percent. The total fertility rate is 3.2 children.

Africa, which makes up 22 percent of the world's land area, has 12 percent of the world's population. Africa has the fastest growing population of any continent in the world. The population is increasing at the rate of 2.9 percent each year. At this rate,

Africa's population of 677 million will double in just 24 years. The life expectancy in Africa, at 54 years, is the lowest of any region. Its total fertility rate, however, at 6.1 children, is by far the highest.

Latin America, which includes the islands of the Caribbean, has over 460 million inhabitants. That is 8 percent of the world's population on 15 percent of the world's land. Although not as heavily populated as Asia and Africa, Latin America's population is growing by 1.9 percent. The overall total fertility rate is 3.2.

Some 72 percent of the people in Latin America live in urban areas. That's more than in any other region in the world. If current trends continue, Mexico City (Mexico) and São Paulo

(Brazil) will be the two largest cities in the world by the year 2000. Mexico City will have 25.6 million inhabitants; São Paulo will have 22.1 million.

Developed Nations Population growth is far slower in the developed nations of North America, Europe, and Japan. In these countries, the growth rate is at or below 1 percent with the total fertility rate at or below the replacement level of 2.1.

The United States, with 260 million people, has the largest population of any industrialized country. It has the third highest population of any country worldwide. The United States has achieved replacement-level fertility. However, the population still has a growth rate of 1 percent. There are two reasons for this. One is that the baby boomers are still in their childbearing years. This has created what demographers refer to as an "echo boom" in the generation born to the baby boomers.

The other reason that the U.S. population is still growing is that the United States attracts immigrants from throughout the world. They come to the United States, a country with a high standard of living, in search of a better life. The population of the United States increases by nearly three million people a year. That increase is the equivalent of adding a city the size of Chicago to the nation's population each year! The U.S. Bureau of the Census predicts that the population will increase by 50 percent by the year 2050. In that year, the population is predicted to be 383 million.

As a group, the nations of Africa now have the highest rates of population growth in the world.

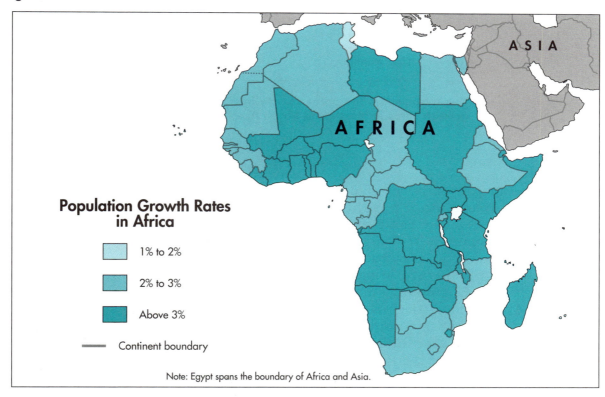

Population Growth Rates in Africa

- 1% to 2%
- 2% to 3%
- Above 3%
- —— Continent boundary

Note: Egypt spans the boundary of Africa and Asia.

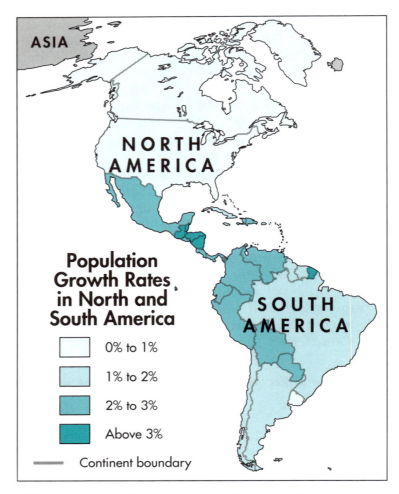

This map shows the great variety in population growth rates in North and South America.

Europe is just 4 percent of the world's land area. Europe has the distinction of being the most densely populated continent. At 513 million, Europe's population is very stable. The average growth rate is only 0.2 percent. A few European countries are even experiencing negative population growth. In these countries, low fertility rates may eventually reduce overall population size.

Russia and the other republics of the former U.S.S.R. add another 285 million people to the world total. They have a small growth rate of 0.6 percent.

The smallest population region of the world is Oceania. This includes Australia. Oceania contributes 28 million to the world's total population.

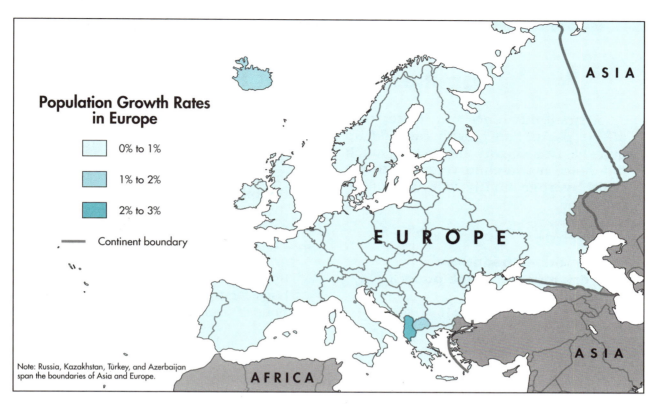

Population Growth Rates in Europe

- 0% to 1%
- 1% to 2%
- 2% to 3%
- —— Continent boundary

Note: Russia, Kazakhstan, Turkey, and Azerbaijan span the boundaries of Asia and Europe.

ASIA

EUROPE

ASIA

AFRICA

Europe has the world's lowest population growth rates.

SECTION REVIEW

1. Explain what is meant by the rule of 70.
2. Describe the population age-structure graph for a population with the largest segment under age 15. Which countries fit this pattern?
3. What is the difference between replacement-level fertility and zero population growth? Can you have one without the other? Explain.
4. What sort of economic problems might a country face if its population is very young—for example, if 40 percent of the individuals are under the age of 15?
5. What sort of economic problems might a country face if its population is rapidly aging—for example, if 20 percent of the individuals are over the age of 60?
6. Which region of the world is home to the greatest number of people? Which is home to the least number of people?

Lab Study

Families of Human Beans

A small difference in a factor that affects population growth can add up quickly. This activity shows how much difference a two-child versus a three-child average family size can make over time.

Materials

Dry kidney beans or dry macaroni (one pound)
Small plastic bags (six per lab group)

Procedure

1. Prepare a plastic bag with two beans to represent parents.
2. Prepare a second bag to represent the offspring in a two-child family (two beans). This is the second generation of beans.
3. Prepare a third bag to represent the grandchildren of generation one (four beans). Continue preparing bags for up to seven more generations of "human" beans.

	NO. OF BEANS 2-CHILD FAMILY	NO. OF BEANS 3-CHILD FAMILY
Generation 1	2	2
Generation 2	2	3
Generation 3	4	9
Generation 4		
Generation 5		
Generation 6		
Generation 7		
Generation 8		
Generation 9		
Generation 10		

4. Assume your beans live for three generations. How many beans will you have "alive" at the end of the activity?
5. Assume a four-generation life span. How many beans will you have alive?
6. Complete the table to show the number of beans after ten generations.
7. Repeat the activity and complete the table for a three-child family pattern.

Conclusion

What difference would it make in the size of the human population if millions of couples decided to have three children instead of two?

For Discussion

1. In Africa, the average family has six children. How much would such a family grow over four generations?
2. Why might a family choose to have three children instead of two?
3. Family-size trends have changed quite a bit in the United States over the past 60 years. They've gone from a two-child average in the 1930s to a four-child average in the late 1950s, and back to a two-child average in the 1990s. What are some reasons for these changes?

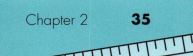

2.3 Population Trends

When will the world's population stop growing? No one knows for certain. Demographers make projections based on available information. The information comes from censuses that most governments in the world conduct. From these censuses, demographers learn the current population. They also learn the age, sex, and some other characteristics of each individual and household.

How do demographers predict future population?

FORECASTING THE NUMBER OF PEOPLE ON EARTH

Present population-age structures tell demographers how populations are likely to grow for the next several generations. Populations with large numbers of young people are expected to grow rapidly. Populations with more even age distributions will grow more slowly.

The rate at which couples use birth-control methods also determines future fertility rates. In most parts of the world greater availability of family-planning services has resulted in lower fertility rates.

To predict future fertility rates, demographers also consider whether governments support family-planning programs. Historically, countries that have really tried to lower birth rates have had great success in slowing population growth.

It is difficult for demographers to predict when certain limiting factors will slow population growth. Such unpredictable factors as famine, epidemics, and wars can raise death rates.

Demographers also consider future life expectancy to predict the earth's

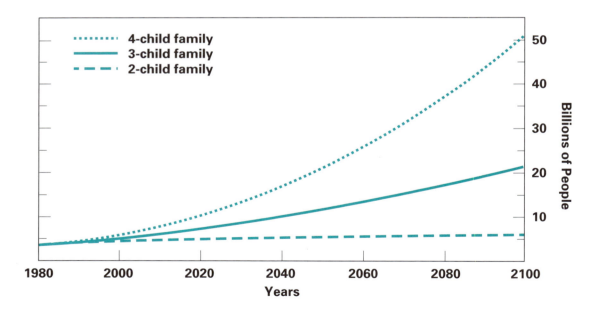

This figure shows population forecasts for the world, based upon average family sizes.

future population. They guess at future life expectancy by looking at present health-care trends.

Because there are so many unpredictable factors, population projections vary widely. Often, demographers make a series of three population projections—low, medium, and high—to cover various possibilities. Demographers currently estimate that the world population will stabilize at between 8 and 15 billion people. They predict that this will happen before the end of the 21st century. Exactly when the population stabilizes will depend on how quickly fertility rates decline.

What are some of the problems of urbanization?

URBANIZATION

As world population has grown, the number and size of urban areas has also increased. There have been massive shifts of population from rural areas to cities. The world, in effect, is in the middle of an urban revolution. When the 20th century began, only one in ten people lived in urban areas. Now nearly one-half of all people live in urban areas. Demographers predict that in the next century more people will live in cities than live on the entire planet today!

In both developed and developing countries, rapid urban growth requires more and more resources to meet people's needs. These resources must come from the areas around the cities. The resources include land, water, and energy.

The 1970 the U.S. Census found that more people in the United States lived in the suburbs than in cities and farms combined. This was the first time in history that this had happened. The number of suburban resi-

dents increased from 35 million in 1950 to more than 120 million in 1990. Today's suburbs extend for dozens of miles from the old city center. They often cover an area 10 to 20 times larger than the city they surround. Automobiles and public transportation have enabled people to live farther from their work places.

In developing countries, the population is still largely rural. More and more people, however, are moving to the cities to find jobs. The growth of population in rural areas has created too much competition for land, water, and food.

Each year, 20 to 30 million of the world's poorest people move from rural to urban areas. They are creating "megacities" in developing countries. The population of some cities in Africa, the least urbanized continent, doubles every 12 years. Some migrants, especially young men, move to cities for a few months each year to add to their family income. The majority, however, stay on and become permanent residents.

In developing countries, a move from country to city often does not improve a person's living conditions. The cities have been unable to meet the needs of their rapidly growing populations. The poor settle in shantytowns. These are groups of crowded, crudely built dwellings on the edges of the city.

What population pressures cause people to leave their homelands?

POPULATION SHIFTS

The term population pressures refers to the problems that result from overcrowding. These problems include

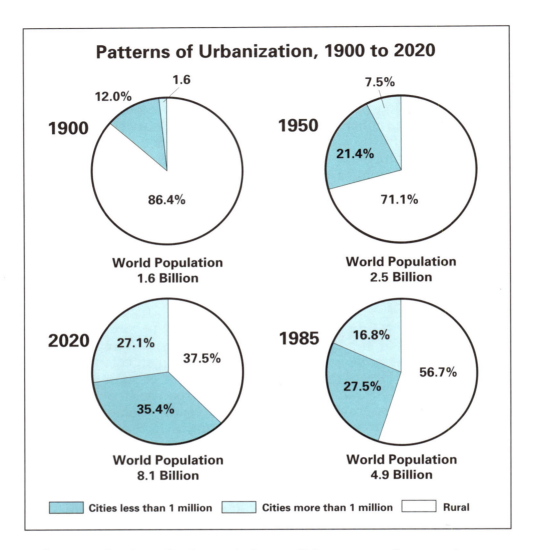

Patterns of Urbanization, 1900 to 2020

1900
1.6
12.0%
86.4%
World Population
1.6 Billion

1950
7.5%
21.4%
71.1%
World Population
2.5 Billion

2020
27.1%
37.5%
35.4%
World Population
8.1 Billion

1985
16.8%
56.7%
27.5%
World Population
4.9 Billion

Cities less than 1 million   Cities more than 1 million   Rural

These graphs show the change in human living patterns from rural to urban environments.

poverty, lack of resources, and too much competition for work. Population pressures throughout the globe have encouraged **migration**. Migration is the movement of people from one place to another. In the case of internal migration, people move from one area of a country to another. An example occurs when people move from rural to urban areas in search of jobs. More commonly, rural people move to other rural areas looking for new land to farm.

Destruction of the environment is the main reason that people move from their homeland. **Environmental refugees** are people who are forced to leave land that can no longer support them. Either natural disasters or misuse has destroyed the land and made it unfit for farming. Environmental refugees have become the single largest category of displaced persons in the world.

Increasing population pressures have forced people in developing countries to try to farm lands that really are not suitable for farming. Such lands are too close to the coast, on steep slopes, or in forested areas. When people try to farm or graze livestock in these fragile areas, they begin a cycle of events that can ruin the land. Once the land can no longer be farmed, families who live off the land must move.

Natural disasters also force people to leave their homes and become environmental refugees. These disasters include droughts, floods, earthquakes, cyclones, volcanoes, tidal waves, and mudslides. Although these are natural events, human activities and population pressures can increase their destructiveness.

For example, millions of Bangladeshi who have no other land to farm live on sandbars in the middle of the Bengal Delta. Every year, ocean tides and monsoon floods wash some of the sandbars away and the Bangladeshi's homes with them. Thousands of slum dwellers in Latin American cities live on hillsides that they have stripped of trees. Heavy rains cause mudslides on these hillsides. When natural disasters strike, thousands of people die and many more are left without homes.

In many cases, people cross borders to find better living conditions in other countries. They hope to find better jobs and a better standard of living in another country. A decision to leave family and homeland behind is rarely easy, but the decision is often a matter of survival.

Most migrants move from developing countries to developed countries. When large numbers of immigrants move to a country, they need food, water, jobs, and services. This places huge demands on the host country's economy and environment. In this way, international migration causes population pressures throughout the world. Even the richest countries find it difficult to take in all the immigrants who want to come. Nonetheless, people in the developing world will most likely keep migrating in search of a better life.

SECTION REVIEW

1. What information do demographers use to make population projections?
2. How does the growth of urban areas affect the surrounding environment?
3. Why do some people become environmental refugees?
4. Why doesn't a move from the country to the city usually bring improved living conditions for people in developing countries?
5. Do you think wealthy countries like the United States should open their doors to environmental, political, and economic refugees from other nations? Why or why not?

Field Study

Making Sense of a Census

Periodically, demographers conduct a census of some population. They gather information on numbers of people, age and sex distribution, racial and ethnic background, marital status, and household data. In this activity, you will take a census of your neighborhood or school community, graph the information, and analyze the data.

Materials

graph paper
colored pencils
calculators (optional)

Procedure

1. Work with a partner. Use the chart provided by your teacher to record the data from your census.
2. Find a sample of at least 50 people (you may use more). Consult with your teacher before deciding which population to choose. Examples of populations for your census include
   - your neighborhood (one or two blocks)
   - several floors of an apartment building
   - the households of your classmates or those of other students in your school
3. Gather and record census data in your chart. First, find out an individual's age. Use the age groups in the first column to find the row that matches the individual's age. Then use the third and fourth columns to record the individuals in your census.

Fill in columns five and six in the chart after you have finished taking census data.

Use the percentages from the table to construct an age-structure graph on graph paper. Use colored pencils or pens to shade the male side one color and the female side a second color.

Conclusions

1. How would you describe the shape of the graph?
2. Do you predict that the population will increase, decrease, or stay the same during the next 20 years? Explain.
3. What difficulties, if any, did you have collecting your data? Why might some people be reluctant to give information to census takers?

For Discussion

If you wanted to start a new business to serve this population, what kind of business might it be? (Think about the kinds of products and services that people of the ages and sexes in your sample might want to buy.)

AGE GROUP	TOTAL #	# OF MALES	# OF FEMALES	% OF MALES	% OF FEMALES
0-4					
5-9					
10-14					
15-19					
20-24					
25-29					
30-34					
35-39					
40-44					
45-49					
50-54					
55-59					
60-64					
65-69					
70-74					
75+					
All				100%	100%

Case Study

Reaching for Zero: Family Planning in Mexico

Marcela Ojeda's eyes still fill with tears when she recalls her arrival in Mexico City in 1972. Marcela and her husband, Atanacio, came to Mexico City to escape the poverty in their home state of Zacatecas. Zacatecas is a rural region—a region of farming and agriculture. Marcela and Atanacio, like many others who were leaving, could no longer grow crops in Zacatecas. The dry land had been used up by constant farming. "We left because we were hungry," Marcela says simply. Near penniless, Marcela and Atanacio

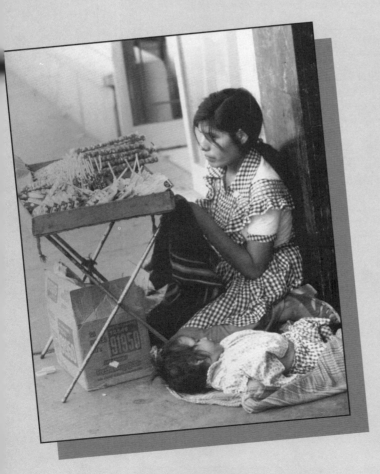

moved to one of Mexico City's spreading slums. Explains Marcela, "We lived in cardboard boxes and foraged for food from the garbage dump."

Mariana Gutierrez describes an equally sad life in Chalco, a huge shantytown in a valley just outside Mexico City. "We had no [electric] light, no water, . . . no nothing," says the 54-year-old mother of 12 children. Mariana clutches the hand of her daughter Rosalba. She remembers a time when her children did not even have fresh water to drink.

Marcela Ojeda and Mariana Gutierrez describe some of the misery caused by Mexico's booming population. Until about 50 years ago, Mexico's population grew at a relatively slow rate. In 1940, the nation's population was approximately 20 million. That is less than one-sixth the population of the United States. By 1990, Mexico's population had risen to more than 85 million. That is one-third the population of the United States.

Today, Mexico's population ranks eleventh in the world. Nowhere is Mexico's population explosion more keenly felt than in its capital, Mexico City. Nearly 800,000 people—the equivalent of San Francisco—move into Mexico City each year. People like Marcela Ojeda, who arrive from rural areas, account for about two-thirds of the growth.

The population explosion has turned Mexico City into the world's largest **metropolitan area.** A metropolitan area consists of a city and its surrounding suburbs. The Mexico City metropolitan area occupies slightly more than 0.2 percent of the nation's land area. It is home, however, to about 22 percent of the nation's population. The huge numbers of people have created gigantic slums nicknamed "lost cities." Without adequate housing and health care, residents refer to themselves as *los perdidos* ("the lost") or *los olvidados* ("the forgotten").

The Mexican government now encourages smaller families. The purpose is to stabilize the growth of the population. The government's target growth rate is 1 percent by the year 2000.

Mexico faces a staggering task. Like most Latin Americans, Mexicans place great value on large, extended families. Also, many people believe that they need a large number of children. Traditionally, children helped families survive by providing more workers for farms and factories.

In the 1970s, many international population agencies thought about the economic reasons for large families. They decided that the population problems of nations like Mexico could be solved by economic development. Economic development would help people out of poverty. They brought water trucks and electricity to shantytowns like Chalco and relieved some of the human misery there.

The population experts soon learned that family-planning decisions were based on more than helping people out of poverty. It took family-planning clinics and easy access to birth control to reduce family size. In cultures that valued large families, people also needed to be convinced of the benefits of family planning.

In 1977, family planners in Mexico found an unusual way to sell family planning to the Mexican people.

That year, millions of Mexicans switched on their televisions to watch a new *telenovela* (soap opera). It was called *"Accompaname"* ("Come Along With Me.")

In daily episodes, the actors in *"Accompaname"* promoted the benefits of family planning. The network conducted a follow-up survey. They found that the series convinced nearly one-half million people to visit family-planning clinics in 1978. This represented a 32 percent increase over the previous year.

The success of *"Accompaname"* inspired two nonprofit groups in the United States to sponsor other public broadcasts. Population Communications International (PCI) helped launch new soap operas. John Hopkins University's Population Communication Services (JHU/PCS) concentrated on reaching Mexican teenagers.

In the 1980s, JHU/PCS organized a massive education-entertainment effort. It was known as the "Communication for Young People Project." In 1986, the project released a record and music video called "Cuando Estemos Juntos" ("When We're Together"). The song featured a duet by a 16-year-old Mexican singer named Tatiana and a 17-year-old Puerto Rican singer named Johnny. Tatiana and Johnny told teenage audiences about the virtues and courage of holding off on sexual relations.

Officials in the Mexican government helped JHU/PCS promote the record. Public radio and TV stations avoided fees if they ended the song with the name and address of family-planning clinics open to teenagers. "Cuando Estemos Juntos" soon hit number one on the pop charts. A few months later, the two singers released

a second song titled "Detente" ("Wait"). Within weeks, it too rose to the top of the charts.

Spokespersons for JHU/PCS estimate that the two songs received about a million hours of free air time. Radio stations played the songs up to 15 times a day for three or four months. At the end of the time, JHU/PCS conducted a survey. The teenagers had a 78 percent recall of the message in "Detente" and a 98 percent recall for "Cuando Estemos Juntos."

But statistics do not tell the whole story. Recall of song lyrics did not directly translate into action. Visits by teenagers to family-planning clinics

increased, but only by about 10 percent. Even so, officials for JHU/PCS view both the soap operas and records as a success. A JHU/PCS official in 1992 explained that family planning was a long process. It was important to keep adding new channels of information.

Mexico's story produced valuable lessons about family planning. To curb fertility rates and population growth, family planners in Mexico identified three important factors. These are government support of family planning, public awareness of the benefits of family planning, and availability of contraceptives.

Since the start of Mexico's new population policy, fertility rates have steadily declined. Between 1972 and 1992, fertility rates fell from an average of 6.2 to 3.8 children per woman. Between 1977 and 1990, use of contraceptives increased from 29 to 53 percent.

Wide differences in fertility rates still exist between rural and urban families. But officials expect rural rates to drop as economic development and family-planning programs extend into the countryside. In 1993, Mexican officials predicted a fertility rate of 3 children per woman within a decade.

International population agencies such as JHU/PCS have applied the lessons learned in Mexico around the world. Soap operas and pop music now advertise family planning from Kenya to Turkey to islands in the Caribbean. Although the global population continues to grow, the rate of growth has slowed. As of 1993, the population of the earth was 5.4 billion—1.6 billion short of a prediction in 1968.

3 CREATING A BALANCE

Nations with rapidly growing populations must plan to meet their future needs for food and other resources.

3.1 Stabilizing Population: A Global Challenge

Many world leaders claim that it is important to bring population size into balance with natural resources. Voluntary family planning can slow the growth of the world's population. Family planning means that parents control the number of children they have.

Over the past 30 years, fertility rates have begun to come down, but they are still high. At current rates, there will still be much population growth well into the next century.

What are some methods that couples can use to control family size?

SLOWING POPULATION GROWTH IS DIFFICULT

Fertility rates decline when couples practice effective family planning.

Family planning includes methods of preventing births. One method is to abstain from sexual activity, especially during days of the month when women are most likely to become pregnant. Another is for couples to use a contraceptive. This can be a device or drug that prevents the male's sperm from fertilizing the female's egg after sexual intercourse.

Eighty-six percent of governments worldwide support national family-planning programs. Yet, there are still 31 countries in the developing world where the vast majority of people have no access to modern family planning. In many countries, lack of funds for these services prevents millions of couples from choosing their family size.

Even when family-planning services are available, couples may choose not to use them. Not every society encourages limiting family size. There are a variety of reasons why couples often choose to have large families. These reasons include religious beliefs about reproduction, as well as cultural traditions about family size

Status of Women   Perhaps the greatest barrier to stabilizing the population is the low status of women in much of the developing world. Fertility rates are high in countries where women are second-class citizens. In these countries, women are denied opportunities that men have. They are denied education, employment, the right to own property, vote, and to hold political office. These women end up in the traditional roles. They have children and work on the farm.

Discrimination against females begins early in many developing countries. In many cultures, couples prefer to have sons because sons take care of their parents in old age.

Daughters marry, and then care for their in-laws, rather than for their own parents. Because of the preference for sons, daughters often receive less health care and nutrition than their brothers. This may lead to poor health and low self-esteem. Only marriage and childbirth, especially of sons, bring women respect in their communities. In many developing countries, women often marry young and begin having children while still children themselves.

According to the World Fertility Survey, 50 percent of African women, 40 percent of Asian women, and 30 percent of Latin American women marry by the age of 18. In fact, the average ages of marriage for females in Bangladesh, Pakistan, and Sierra Leone are only 11.6, 15.3, and 15.6, respectively. Men marry at older ages.

Cultural traditions   Cultural traditions also limit women's access to employment. Women perform two-thirds of the world's work, mostly in the home and field. Women, however, earn only one-tenth of the world's income. In every country, there are less women than men in the paid-labor force.

Greater economic independence encourages women to have fewer children. In industrialized countries, fertility rates have declined as women have had more opportunities for employment. The status of women will be very important in determining future population growth rates.

Lack of Education   In countries throughout the world, fertility rates always drop when women are given more education. Yet currently, 50 percent of women in developing countries are illiterate, or unable to read. Only 32 percent of men are illiterate. In many African and South Asian coun-

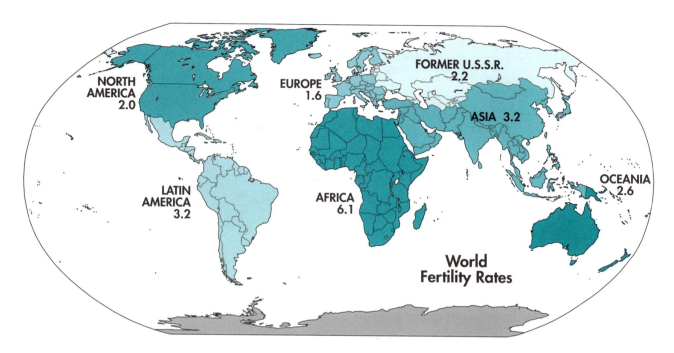

This map shows fertility rates for seven world regions. The rates show the average number of children born to women.

tries, four out of five women over 25 years of age have had no schooling. Parents tend to send their sons to school and keep their daughters home to help with chores.

The education of girls and women is closely linked with a society's average family size. In Brazil, for instance, uneducated women have an average of 6.5 children each. Women who have completed high school average only 2.5 children. In Liberia, women who have been to high school are ten times more likely to use contraceptives than women who have never been to school at all.

The education of women results in lower birth rates, later marriages, improved family health, and a dramatic decrease in infant mortality. The United Nations has launched a campaign to eliminate women's illiteracy by the year 2000.

In many developing countries, men's status rests on how many children they have. Men want a lot of sons to inherit the family property, continue the family name, and support them in old age. These traditions create some male resistance to family planning in developing countries. It is important to educate men and women about the connections between smaller families and a better standard of living.

Infant mortality Family-planning programs best lower fertility rates when they are part of an effort to improve health in general. Couples have more children when they fear losing them to disease and poor nutrition.

Fear of contraceptives Sometimes, men and women reject contraceptives for fear of dangerous side effects. Rumor and gossip can create widespread fear. For instance, 50 percent of Filipino women

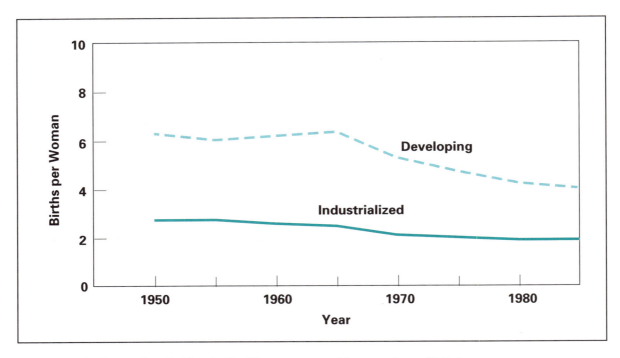

This graph shows the decline in fertility, measured by number of births per woman, for developing nations of the world. Notice that the difference between developing and industrialized nations has become smaller.

believe that birth-control pills cause sterility. A third of Chilean women think the pills accumulate in the stomach and cause cancer. A third of Moroccan women blame them for causing birth defects. Family-planning services must include accurate information about birth control.

SECTION REVIEW

1. Name and describe three methods by which a couple can control family size.
2. How does education affect population growth?
3. What are some reasons that might explain why men and women in the United States do not practice family planning?
4. State three reasons why governments might want to provide good family-planning services for their people.

You Solve It

Imagine you have just been appointed the new minister of population by the president of a developing country. The growing population threatens to overwhelm the country's natural resources. The president has asked you to outline a plan to lower the birth rate over the next ten years. Here are some facts about the country:

- It has a growth rate of 3 percent per year.
- Only 20 percent of the people use some form of contraception.
- A number of industrialized countries have promised money to help you start a population program.
- Most of the population is rural and lives by farming.
- Women are responsible for all of the work around the house and much of it in the field.
- Women go to school only one or two years, and only 15 percent of the women can read.
- Most women marry by age 16 and begin bearing children soon after.
- Nearly 1 in 10 children die as infants, and about 1 in 100 women die as a result of childbirth.
- All the paid work goes to men.
- Men rely on their sons to support them in old age. There is no national social security system.
- Television is becoming a popular means of entertainment.
- Most households own a radio.

With a partner, propose a population program for the next ten years by selecting ideas from the options below or by thinking of other ideas yourself. Be prepared to offer reasons for your selections. Put your family-planning proposal in writing so that it is ready to give to the president of the country.

Options

1. Set up family-planning clinics in all communities of 1,000 or more residents.
2. Require that boys and girls stay in school through the 6th grade.
3. Advertise contraceptives on radio and TV.
4. Show U.S. soap operas on TV.
5. Train people in each community to distribute contraceptives and family-planning information to adults.
6. Raise the minimum age of marriage to 21.
7. Make jobs outside the home available to women.
8. Propose to the government that the nation grant women equal rights.
9. Require that couples who have more than two children pay an extra tax.
10. Invest money to help women start up small businesses.
11. Set up a social security program.
12. Teach sex education beginning in elementary school.
13. Offer seminars on why smaller families are better for the economy.
14. Budget more money for children's immunization against common diseases.

3.2 Family-Planning Programs: A Global View

Thanks in part to family-planning programs, fertility rates are declining.

SENDING THE MESSAGE

Successful family-planning programs usually include efforts to change people's ideas about family planning. These include multimedia campaigns using radio and TV. Millions of viewers in Mexico, India, Pakistan, Nigeria, Kenya, Egypt, and Turkey have tuned into TV soaps that include family-planning ideas.

In Zimbabwe, radios are more common than TVs. Here, a radio show that aired in 1988 and 1989 countered traditional male attitudes toward family planning. "Akaruma Nechekuchera" ("You Reap What You Sow") told of Jonas, a poor villager with two wives and 15 children.

Family-planning promoters also get their message across through advertising. They use TV spots, feature-length films, and music videos. Teen superstars in Mexico and the Philippines encourage sexual responsibility through the lyrics of songs and music videos. In the case study, you read about "Detente" ("Wait"), a hit song in Mexico. In this song, Tatiana and Johnny urge young listeners to postpone sexual relations. The song says that "love on the run creates bread- and-water children." Surveys show that teens throughout Mexico discussed the song's messages with parents and friends.

SUCCESSFUL FAMILY PLANNING PROGRAMS

Colombia, South America, Indonesia, Asia, and Zimbabwe, Africa are examples of countries with successful programs.

Colombia   In Colombia, community volunteers bring family-planning services to the people. *Profamilia*, the country's family-planning association, trains instructors. The instructors, in turn, train representatives in each community to serve as resource people. In every town and village, men and women know who to see for information and contraceptives. *Profamilia* also cooperates with pharmacies, general stores, and supermarkets to distribute contraceptives at low prices. *Profamilia's* approach of reaching out to every community with the help of trusted local women has paid off. The fertility rate has dropped from over 7 children in 1965 to just 2.8 in 1993.

Colombia's system has been copied throughout the world. Countries that now use it include Mexico, Thailand, Brazil, and Indonesia. These countries make an effort to provide rural residents with health services even if they don't have clinics and physicians.

Indonesia   Indonesia, Asia, is a string of 13,000 islands with many waterways. Many communities are not served by roads. Indonesia has established "floating clinics." These are located on boats that navigate the waterways. Use of contraceptives has grown five times in the last 20 years. Today, knowledge of family planning is almost universal in Indonesia. Most young people want only two children.

Zimbabwe   Zimbabwe, in Africa, distributes family-planning information in rural communities. The "grannies for family planning" program uses women of good standing in the community who have had at least seven years of schooling. They are trained for three months to serve as

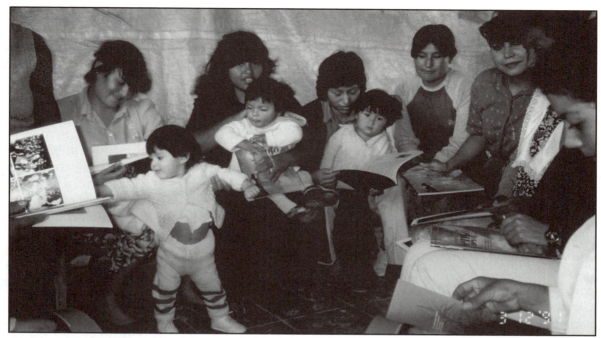

An increasing number of adults around the world are participating in family planning sessions, such as the one pictured above in Mexico.

family-planning workers in rural communities. These women are equipped with bicycles and backpacks, with condoms and other contraceptives. Zimbabwe has tripled its rate of contraceptive use among parents in less than a decade.

Zimbabwe is now a family-planning model for other African countries. The government of Zimbabwe has also tried to improve women's educational and legal status and to expand basic health-care services. These efforts have contributed to Zimbabwe's success.

FAMILY PLANNING IN LARGE NATIONS

China's One-child Policy No population program has been more controversial than China's. Until recent decades, China had one of the highest rates of population growth in the world. By the early 1960s, a famine had claimed the lives of 30 million Chinese people. It was clear that the country could no longer feed its rapidly growing population. Too little land and water were left for farming. In 1971, China's leaders launched a national campaign to slow population growth.

The campaign was known as *wan-xi-shao*, "later-longer-fewer." The program promoted late marriages, long intervals between births, and a two-child family. The program led to a great reduction in the fertility rate. Rates dropped from six children per family in the 1960s to three by 1979. However, demographers still predicted that China's population would be 1.8 billion by the year 2000. The country's carrying capacity was estimated at 700 million.

Therefore, in 1979, China's leaders started a "one-family, one-child" campaign. They introduced a system of rewards and penalties to encourage one-child families. A couple who pledged to have just one child might be rewarded with land, better housing, jobs, and schooling for the child. A couple that had more than one child might have high fines and lower wages.

Later, China's plan began to draw international attention. There were disturbing reports of some forced abortions, or terminations of pregnancy. There were also reports of forced sterilizations by local officials. No one knows how widespread the practices were.

By 1993, China's population had grown to 1.2 billion. Fertility rates had fallen to just under two children per family. China is home to over one-fifth of all the people of the world. Therefore, the success of China's population program will be important in determining global population growth.

Family Planning in the United States   The United States supports family-planning programs. In the United States, more than 70 percent of the population uses contraceptives. Most people have access to family-planning information and services. The services come from government programs and private organizations. Compared to other industrialized countries, though, the United States lags in some areas of family-planning. It does not provide all young people with sex education and family planning services. The nation has higher teenage-pregnancy rates than do other developed countries. More than one million American teenage women become pregnant each year.

SECTION REVIEW

1. Why might a woman in a developing country feel more comfortable getting family-planning advice from a local person than from a physician at a clinic in a neighboring city?

2. Why do you think China's one-child policy was criticized by people in other nations?

3. How might family life differ in a society where most couples have one child than in a society where most couples have two or three children?

4. How might giving more money now to developing countries to slow the growth of their populations save developed countries money in the long run?

You Solve It

Below are sets of demographic data for two very different countries, Japan and Brazil. Both have had much population change in the 20th century. By analyzing the demographics of the countries, you can appreciate the decisions that their leaders need to make to plan for their people.

Vital Statistics (1993):

BRAZIL
Population: 152 million (5th largest population worldwide)
Land area: 3,265,060 square miles
Birth rate: 23 per 1,000
Death rate: 7 per 1,000
Growth rate: 1.5 percent
Doubling time: 46 years
Infant mortality rate: 63 per 1,000
Life expectancy: 67 years
Total fertility rate: 2.6

JAPAN
Population: 125 million (7th largest population worldwide)
Land area: 145,370 square miles
Birth rate: 10 per 1,000
Death rate: 7 per 1,000
Growth rate: 0.3 percent
Doubling time: 217 years
Infant mortality rate: 4 per 1,000
Life expectancy: 76 years
Total fertility rate: 1.5

Work in cooperative learning groups of four and in pairs of two within each group. With your group, decide which pair will focus on Japan, which on Brazil.

With your partner, use the data from the table to create an age-structure graph for the country you are focusing on: either Japan or Brazil. (See examples of age-structure graphs in Chapter 2, page 27.) Shade the male side of your graph with one color; the female side with a different color.

Share your graph with the other members of your group. Draw conclusions together.

How would you describe the shape of each country's graph? What does this shape tell you about each country's demographic history?

List five products and five services that might be in demand now, given the age-sex distribution in each country. Put a plus sign (+) next to the ones for which the demand will probably increase in the next 20 years. Put a minus sign (-) next to the ones for which the demand will probably decrease in the next 20 years.

If the present growth rates continue, what concerns might each government have about its work force?

From what you know about the countries' geography and land areas, what problems will they probably face if population grows?

What historical event might explain the bulge in the middle of Japan's graph and the related lower bulge? Can you think of any other countries that might have a similar demographic history?

Which country will probably need to hire more teachers within the next 10 years? Which country will probably need more health services for the elderly?

Food production in industrialized countries is supported by advanced machinery.

seeable future. Examples are coal and oil. People are using up some renewable resources faster than the resources can replace themselves. People are also consuming some nonrenewable resource that can never replace themselves.

Consumption of resources is linked to wealth. Slightly over one billion people are rich by global standards. About three billion people are neither rich nor poor. Slightly over one billion people are poor. As a result, consumption varies greatly from one part of the world to another.

In the richest countries, people tend to purchase the things they need and want without much regard to how they are using up natural resources. In countries that are neither rich nor poor, people buy what they need but seldom can afford luxuries. In the poorest countries, people often grow, hunt, or make things rather than buy them.

3.3 Human Populations and Food

Humans have some advantages over other species. They have problem-solving skills and the ability to manipulate tools. With these advantages, humans create technologies that help them meet their basic needs and live more comfortably. Yet, our use of these technologies is using up the natural resources that humans depend on.

There are two types of natural resources: renewable and nonrenewable. **Renewable resources** can replace themselves—trees are an example. **Nonrenewable resources** cannot replace themselves in the fore-

What problems have been caused by food production in industrialized countries?

FOOD PRODUCTION IN INDUSTRIALIZED COUNTRIES

People in industrialized and developing countries meet their need for food in different ways. Methods of agriculture often depend on how much money farmers can spend on seeds, machinery, fuel, fertilizer, pesticides, and irrigation.

Family farms used to produce a variety of crops. The farmers would feed their families and sell the rest in the market. In industrialized countries, there are fewer and fewer general family farms. Increasingly, small farmers have left their farms for work in the cities, where life may be easier and income more reliable.

Today, most food in industrialized countries comes from large commercial farms. These large farms usually specialize in just one or two products—for example, corn, wheat, and beef, or cotton and soybeans. The large farms use the techniques developed in the Green Revolution.

The raising of animals for food also occurs on a large scale with the help of technology. Chickens and eggs, for example, no longer come from a coop behind the farmer's home. Today, indoor factories raise more than 100,000 chickens at a time. They are fed and given water by machine.

Governments in industrialized countries often support prices and provide services that encourage huge, specialized farms. Services include agricultural research and improved storage facilities. The agricultural production that results is so high that there are sometimes surpluses of food.

The new technologies have significantly increased global food production. They have also taken a toll on the natural environment. They have caused increased erosion and water contamination by fertilizers and pesticides.

Other environmental problems are caused by the food packaging used in industrialized countries. Packaging protects food, allows it to be easily stacked in stores, and makes it attractive to the shopper. But it can also be quite wasteful. Almost half of all paper produced and almost one-fourth of all plastics are used for packaging. Much of the packaging is thrown away after a single use. Production of packaging and disposal of wastes consume resources and contribute to pollution.

In industrialized countries, per-person consumption of food is high. Many people's diets are so rich that the diets actually cause health risks. These diets are likely to include much more animal protein from meat, eggs, and dairy products than the diets of people in developing countries do. The average person in the United States consumes 112 kilograms of meat annually. The average French or German person consumes 90 kilograms a year. The average Chinese eats only 24 kilograms of meat a year, and the average Indian, just 2.

These unhealthy diets actually use up many more natural resources than healthy diets. For example, 2,500 pounds of corn and 350 pounds of soybeans might be used in raising an 80-pound calf. This calf produces 1,000 seven-ounce servings of meat. The same grains that fed the calf, baked into breads and casseroles, could provide 18,000 eight-ounce servings rich in plant protein! This is why the food consumption habits of industrialized countries often seem wasteful to people in other parts of the world.

How is agriculture in developing countries different from agriculture in developed countries?

FOOD PRODUCTION IN DEVELOPING COUNTRIES

In developing countries, agricultural practices vary. There are some large, modern farming operations, but there are many small, traditional farms. Green Revolution technologies are expensive. Moreover, to use them, farmers need technical help, loans to

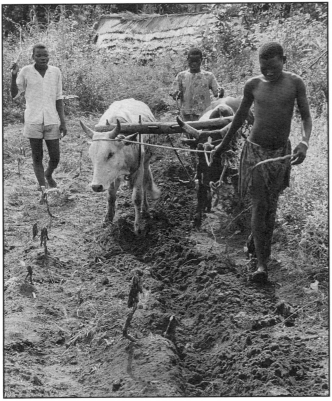

Most farmers in poor nations, such as these men in the African nation of Dahomey, cannot afford new farm machines.

on their own muscles or animal power to work the land. Many of their tools and techniques have been used since ancient times.

As the population of developing nations grows and modern agriculture moves in, relatively few people end up owning more and more of the land. Increasing numbers of people find themselves without jobs or good land to farm. Some of these people go to the cities in search of work. Often, it is the men who go, while the women stay behind, caring for the children and farming. Women are one-third to one-half of all agricultural laborers in developing countries.

Yet in many developing countries, women are not permitted to own land. They cannot take advantage of training programs. They are denied the loans they need to buy supplies. Their low social status makes it difficult for them to improve their farming techniques. To make matters worse, governments in developing countries put money into growing crops they can export. These are crops like coffee or sugarcane. The government doesn't help with subsistence crops, such as cassava, that provide the "daily bread" for women and their families.

Many rural people, in desperation, try to farm or graze livestock on land that is not good for farming or grazing. This often destroys the land. In struggling to survive, the poor are forced to destroy the natural resources on which their future life depends.

Furthermore, governments in developing countries keep prices of food products very low to help the urban poor. These prices discourage farmers from investing in conservation techniques that could help them produce more food.

buy supplies, and access to markets where they can sell their increased harvests. Therefore, these technologies are out of reach to most of the world's food growers who are not already using them.

The vast majority of the world's farmers still practice traditional agriculture. Between 80 and 90 percent of the people in poor countries live in rural areas and depend on **subsistence agriculture.** Subsistence agriculture is farming to meet the farmer's own survival needs. Subsistence farmers lack money to invest in modern agricultural technologies. They use fewer and smaller machines. They rely

SECTION REVIEW

1. Explain the difference between renewable and nonrenewable resources.
2. Name two traditional agricultural techniques that are being used again in both industrialized and developing countries. Describe the problems they help prevent or solve.
3. List four of your favorite foods. Then complete the following steps:
   a. Put a check next to the foods made from other ingredients.
   b. For each checked item, list the ingredients you think went into making the food.
   c. Rank your foods from 1 to 4. A 1 refers to the food it takes the least resources to produce; 4, the most.
   d. Analyze your ranking. In general, do you prefer foods that many of the world's people could afford to eat or those that only a few could afford?

You Solve It

It is easy to become overwhelmed by the environmental challenges facing our globe. But there are steps that individuals can take. In this activity, you will explore the way global challenges translate into local challenges.

Your teacher will give you a copy of the "Think Globally, Act Locally" chart. Look at it carefully. Note that columns include global challenges, local challenges, and ideas for personal action.

For each global challenge, complete the following steps:

- Read the related local challenges and ideas for personal actions.
- Add one or two of your own ideas to the list of personal actions in column
- For each personal action on the list, note in column 4 whether the action will be easy, average, or difficult for a person to do.
- In column 5, note whether the action will be unlikely, somewhat likely, or very likely to be effective in helping to meet the challenge.

Put a check mark next to two personal actions in column 3 that you feel you would be willing and able to do.

Keep a journal for at least the next four weeks in which you make notes on your progress in the actions you chose.

Some personal actions contribute to the solution of more than one problem. For example, using a car less often helps reduce air pollution, reduces factors leading to climate change, and conserves energy. Describe how some actions on the list help solve more than one problem.

Some personal actions help solve one problem but contribute to another. For example, switching from disposable to cloth diapers helps reduce waste but requires the use of large amounts of water and energy to wash diapers. Describe how some actions on the list solve one problem but contribute to another.

4 HUMAN IMPACT ON NATURAL ECOSYSTEMS

Natural resources, such as this forest, are being used up at a faster rate due to the needs of the growing human population on earth.

4.1 Wild Lands Vanish

As the human population grows, more and more wild lands are being used to meet human needs. The 93 million people added to the world's population each year require food, clothing, and shelter. They also need land for factories, stores, schools, office buildings, roads, and recreational facilities.

To meet human needs, wild lands are often cleared of growth. The soil may be leveled or reshaped for new uses. The waters of wild rivers may be used for drinking, irrigation, and industry. Every time humans use a wild land, its ecosystem changes dramatically.

The "taming" of wild lands is happening on a large scale now. Every month, a number of people roughly equal to New York City is added to the world! The added human activity not only affects wild life but also the quality of air, water, and soil. These are resources all living things depend on.

CLEARING FORESTS

To meet the needs of the growing human population, forests are being used at a rapid pace. Only about 40 percent of the approximately 6,750,000 square miles of forest that once covered the planet remains. The rest has been cut down to meet people's growing needs for wood and land.

Wood is a material that is widely used to meet two of the most basic human needs: fuel and shelter. Wood is used as a building material throughout the world. Nearly half the world's people depend on wood as a fuel to cook their food and heat their homes. In addition, wood is used to make furniture, paper, synthetic fibers, and many chemical products. Forests are also cleared so that people can use the land to grow crops, graze livestock, or build housing and roads.

Tropical forests are very important to the world's environment. But approximately 100 acres of tropical forests are destroyed every minute! It is estimated that in Asia, Africa, and Central and South America, the planet loses 51 acres of rain forest every year because of human use. This is an area the size of Pennsylvania.

Clearing forests has serious effects on the water supply. Spongy soils in forests soak up rain, The water seeps gradually down into the ground and becomes streams that flow even in dry weather. When trees are cut, the soil is no longer sheltered from the sun and wind. It erodes easily. Then the rain runs off quickly. The water isn't absorbed by the soil, and the chances of drought and flooding increase.

Deforestation, or the loss of forests, in the tropics may also be changing the world's climate. Tropical rain forests, which are mostly near the equator, absorb a great deal of heat. This creates a band of hot rising air around the equator. The massive uprising is partly responsible for the circulation patterns of air over the entire globe. When deforestation in the tropics disrupts this process, the result can change the climate patterns of the world. For example, there may be less rainfall over large portions of the globe.

Deforestation even alters the very makeup of the atmosphere. Trees take carbon dioxide from the air and replace it with oxygen through the process of photosynthesis. When there are fewer trees, the level of carbon dioxide in the atmosphere increases. This has been happening steadily.

What are the impacts of overgrazing?

OVERGRAZING GRASSLANDS

Animals graze, or feed on grasses, on about one-fourth of the earth's land. These animals provide meat, milk products, leather, and fur for millions of people. As the number of humans increases, so does the need for animal products. This leads to larger herds of livestock. More livestock need more land for grazing. If that is not possible, the livestock need to eat more of the vegetation on the land that is available. This is known as **overgrazing**. The growing human population needs more land for many uses. Therefore, instead of spreading out to more grasslands, livestock often overgraze the grasslands on which they feed.

People need to manage livestock herds carefully to prevent overgrazing.

In addition, lands that are barely suitable for grazing are being used for grazing anyway. When people graze too many animals on the land, the nutritious grasses can be entirely used up. Weeds replace the grasses, and weeds will not adequately feed the livestock or anchor the soil.

Eventually, shrubs may move in and replace the grasses as the main type of vegetation. Fires that used to keep down the number of shrubs no longer burn because the grasses that provided their fuel are gone. As the plant species disappear, the variety of animal life in the area decreases.

Another effect of overgrazing is that the soil is less able to retain moisture. The hooves of animals trample down soil, making it harder and more compact. Compact soil is less able to hold moisture. Then wind and water easily erode the dry topsoil. The soil that washes away may clog streams which, in turn, may cause flooding. The water table may fall because the rain can't seep through the soil to refill it. In dry climates, grazing lands turn to dust as the wind blows the topsoil away.

Overgrazing, then, is an important cause of the decline in usefulness of soil. Worldwide, overgrazing affects some 6.8 million square kilometers (2.6 million square miles) of land. That's an area about three-fourths the size of the United States.

As grasslands become overused in every part of the world, they can no longer support increased production of beef and mutton. From 1950 to 1987, global meat production per person rose from 18 kilograms to 32 (or from about 39 to about 70 pounds). But since 1987, meat production per person has not increased at all.

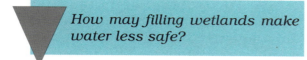

How may filling wetlands make water less safe?

FILLING WETLANDS

One way in which people try to make wild lands suitable for human use is by filling or dredging wetlands. Wetlands are swamps, marshes, or bogs where water naturally saturates the soil most of the year. About 54 percent of the wetlands that used to exist in the United States have been purposely filled with sand or soil or dredged. When filled, they are used for agriculture, industry, shopping malls, housing, or other development. When dredged, or deepened, they are used for transportation or other purposes.

Wetlands have unique ecosystems. The plants in wetlands are unusual. They can stand having their roots underwater for long periods. Wetlands are the homes for many different types of wildlife. They also are the breeding grounds for some animals. The National Audubon Society estimates that about 150 kinds of birds and 200 kinds of fish depend on wetland ecosystems.

Filling wetlands changes them significantly. Their populations of wildlife decline severely. Among species that

When natural wetlands, such as the one above, are dredged or filled, our water quality declines, and wildlife populations disappear.

are endangered in the United States, about 45 percent of the animal species and 25 percent of the plants depend on wetlands for their homes.

The use of wetlands also has an effect on water flow and quality. Wetlands are valuable for their ability to hold excess water. This helps to control flooding and slows the erosion of soil. In addition, wetlands act as natural purifiers of water. Like great sponges, their soils remove sediments, impurities, and excess nutrients from the water. The plentiful algae and bacteria take up minerals and break down other organic matter.

Destroying wetlands means reducing this natural filtering process. Ultimately, this may make the water less safe for both wildlife and human beings. Destroying wetlands also removes the giant spongy buffers that guard against flooding and erosion during major storms. The effects of the destruction of wetlands were dramatically seen in the midwestern United States in the summer of 1993. Heavy rains caused the Mississippi and Missouri rivers to overflow and flood massive areas in several states. The flooding caused billions of dollars worth of damage. Some of the worst flooding occurred in Iowa, Missouri, and Illinois. These states have lost, respectively, 89 percent, 87 percent, and 85 percent of their wetlands over the years. They lost them because people built levees to hold back the water so that the land could be used for farming.

SECTION REVIEW

1. The United States Forest Service administers the country's 191 million acres of national forests. By law, the forests are "for outdoor recreation, range, timber, watershed, and wildlife and fish purposes." Are there times when people's use of the forest for one of these purposes works directly against its use for another purpose? Describe two examples of situations where this might be a problem.

2. Many people have wished that mosquitoes could be done away with once and for all. What means might people use to try to kill off the mosquito population? If they succeed, what might be the effects on other species?

3. Most people in the United States use forest products and livestock products. They, therefore, contribute to the market demands that lead to human effects on ecosystems. Make a list of forest products that you use in your home or school. Put a check next to any item(s) on your lists that you think you might be able to use less of, or use less often, to help protect natural ecosystems. Repeat for livestock products.

You Solve It

"Everything is connected to everything else" is often considered the First Law of Ecology. In this activity, you will work with a partner to explore connections between the human population and the natural and social environment.

With your partner, write the words "MORE PEOPLE" in the center of a sheet of paper. Draw a circle around the words. This circle represents the growing population in most countries of the world, including the United States.

Now consider what "MORE PEOPLE" might mean for the physical environment and for society. Consider positives, negatives, and neutral effects (examples: "MORE HOUSES," "MORE CREATIVE GENIUSES"). Write these effects around your original circle. Connect each effect to your original circle (the cause) with a cause-and-effect arrow. Then draw a circle around all the effects.

Consider the possible effect of each item in your outer circle. For example, "MORE HOUSES" might mean "FEWER TREES." "MORE CREATIVE GENIUSES" might lead to "NEW TECHNOLOGICAL DISCOVERIES." Write these effects around the outer circle. Then draw a circle around them, and connect them with arrows to show cause and effect. Don't worry if your arrows cross and your "wheel" begins to look more like a web.

Optional: Make a large poster showing the relationships in your "wheel" in a colorful way. Ask if it can be displayed on your classroom wall, in a library display case, or in a store's display window to boost other people's ecological awareness.

Analyze the cause-and-effect relationships you have identified. Would each necessarily have to lead to the effect you identified? For example, would "MORE PEOPLE" have to have "MORE HOUSES," or might larger numbers of people live in the same house? Explain.

Choose three cause-and-effect relationships in your diagram that would not actually have to happen the way you showed them. Explain how each might lead to a different effect than the one you originally identified.

4.2 Effects on the Earth's Life-Support Systems

Air, water, and soil are the basic building blocks that sustain all life. Every time humans change an ecosystem, they are changing these building blocks. Though each change may seem small, altogether they add up to a significant effect. The changes affect not only populations of wildlife but ultimately of humans as well.

Why is the loss of topsoil harmful to both plants and animals?

AGRICULTURE'S EFFECTS ON SOIL

In the 1960s, researchers developed new techniques of agriculture.

Pesticides sprayed on crops can improve the size of the harvest but are expensive to use.

Their goal was to feed the world's increasing human population. They wanted to deal with hunger and malnutrition in developing countries. New strains of grain, such as rice, wheat, and corn, were developed.

The new grains vastly increased the production of food in many countries. In fact, between 1950 and the late 1980s, while the world's population doubled, its food production almost tripled. Growing these improved grains, however, requires large amounts of water, fertilizer, and chemical pesticides. This is more expensive than people originally thought it would be.

Irrigation is necessary to grow these grains in many areas. But irrigation leaves salts and other chemicals in the soil. Without proper drainage, the chemicals may accumulate to poisonous levels. Fertilizers and pesticides are significant sources of water pollution.

As a result, the new agricultural techniques change the soil over the years. The soil may become increasingly less fertile, which gradually reduces harvests. There are signs that this is already happening. Production of grain increased about 3 percent per year from 1950 to 1984. However, it has increased only about 1 percent per year since then. This is slower than the rate of human population growth.

There is another way that agriculture often affects soil. When land is deeply plowed, the topsoil erodes. Topsoil is especially important because it is rich in the decomposed remains of living things. Topsoil provides the nutrients that are the basis of life for most plant species. Plants species, in turn, feed animal species and humans. Between farming and deforestation, an estimated 25 billion tons of topsoil are lost each year.

HUMAN EFFECTS ON AIR

Throughout the United States and in many other parts of the world, air pollution offends people. They sense that human activity has affected the air beyond its limits. In many places, it is actually dangerous to breathe! The World Health Organization monitors air quality. They estimate that 70 percent of the world's urban population breathes air that sometimes contains unhealthy levels of pollution. Another 10 percent breathes "marginal" air.

All air contains some natural pollutants, such as pollen, dust, and volcanic ash. But human activity is responsible for most air pollution. The three major causes of air pollution are use of energy, emissions of motor vehicles, and industrial production. All three increase as the human population increases.

Increasing numbers of people need heat, light, and electricity for their homes. When fossil fuels such as coal and oil are burned to meet these needs, pollutants spread into the air. Cities often burn trash. This adds more pollutants to the air. Exhaust from people's cars and trucks adds pollutants. Power plants and factories add pollutants.

It is little wonder that large cities have particularly serious air pollution. Cities are densely populated. Human and industrial activity is very concentrated there. Polluted air is a particular problem in the cities of developing countries. These cities are trying to industrialize rapidly. Unlike most developed countries, they are making few or no efforts to prevent pollution.

In developing countries, human activity contaminates the indoor air as well. In rural areas, people tend to burn coal or **biomass fuels** to cook their food and heat their homes. Biomass fuels are those that come from plants or from animal wastes. They include wood, crop wastes, and animal dung. About two-thirds of the world's people burn these traditional biomass fuels. They frequently use stoves with poor ventilation or no ventilation. This often leads to accumulations of poisonous substances in the air in their houses. This poses serious risks to health.

Acid Rain   Air pollutants that endanger human health affect plants and animals too. Particularly harmful is **acid rain** (and snow and fog). Acid rain forms when fossil fuels burn and give off the acids sulfur dioxide and nitrous oxide. Acid rain is a major cause of the decrease in crops and forests in Europe and North America. China is also beginning to experience acid rain problems in its southern provinces. High acid levels in bodies of water affect fish and other life forms in water. Sometimes, the wildlife dies off entirely.

Greenhouse Gases   Air pollution produced by human activity may be changing the climate of the entire world. The atmosphere may be warming up, like a giant greenhouse. The greenhouse effect works in the following way. Sunlight passes through the atmosphere to warm the earth's surface. The earth, and objects on it, radiate, or give off, some of the sun's energy as infrared rays (heat). Some of those rays escape into space. But some heat is trapped by water vapor, carbon dioxide, methane, and other gases in the atmosphere. These are called **greenhouse gases.**

There is a clear connection between human population growth and

The air quality in the world's cities is often poor. Denver, shown here, has air polluted by burning fossil fuel.

increasing concentrations of greenhouse gases in the air. Recently, scientists studied carbon dioxide in the air. They found a nearly perfect match over 25 years between carbon dioxide increases in the atmosphere and world population growth. The match was so good that it suggested that population growth could be estimated by measuring carbon dioxide in the air instead of taking a census.

How much of the earth's water is fresh water?

HUMAN EFFECTS ON WATER

People depend on clean water as much as they do on clean air. But the demand for water rises along with the world's population. Over the past three centuries, human use of water has grown more than 35 times. During just the last 30 years, the demand for water has doubled in about half the countries in the world. The result is a shortage of water in many parts of the world. According to a UN report, 80 countries suffer serious water shortages. These countries make up 40 percent of the world's population. It is estimated that 1.2 billion people do not have safe water. Efforts to supply safe water are falling behind human population growth rates.

Fresh water comes from surface water in lakes, rivers, streams, and reservoirs. It also comes from groundwater in underground supplies called aquifers. People use fresh water for domestic purposes, such as drinking, cooking, and washing. People also use fresh water for industrial uses. These include agriculture, manufacturing, food processing, and generating electricity.

Irrigation and other agricultural needs use the largest share of the world's fresh water. Agriculture accounts for 69 percent of all the fresh water used. Industry accounts for another 23 percent. Domestic use (washing, drinking, cooking) accounts for 8 percent.

Most of the earth's total water is saltwater. Just 3 percent is fresh water. Only a tiny portion of that 3 percent is available for people to use. Most of it—79 percent—is locked up in polar ice and glaciers. The rest is—like the human population—unevenly distributed around the globe.

As a result, some regions have very serious water shortages. East and West Africa usually have water shortages. In the Middle East and North Africa, where there are many political difficulties, water shortages add to the problems. China also is finding that its use of water is greater than its supplies in many areas. China anticipates water shortages in 450 of the country's 644 cities by the year 2000.

Many people in poor nations do not have a modern source of safe drinking water.

SECTION REVIEW

1. State at least two ways in which human activities affect each of these life-support systems of the earth: (a) soil, (b) air, (c) water
2. How have your own activities affected the air, water, and land today? To answer, list
   a. things you have done today that have used energy
   b. ways in which you have used water today
   c. foods you have eaten that come from crops or livestock
   d. clothing fabrics you have worn today that come from crops or livestock
3. Human activities cause changes in air, water, and soil. State at least three ways in which people's health may be harmed by these changes.
4. Has your own health ever been affected by pollution of the air, water, or soil? If so, how?

You Solve It

If the human population of the world continues to grow at the current rate, there will be twice as many people on earth in approximately 40 years. Doubling the number of people will affect the air, water, soil, plants, animals, and even the climate. In this activity, you will think about the local effect.

Imagine twice as many people using your local park. Predict the effect on the park's ecosystems.

Imagine twice as many people driving cars on the streets of your neighborhood. Predict the effects on your neighborhood's environment.

Imagine twice as many people living in your city or town. Predict the effects on:
- the natural environment
- the quality of life (taking into consideration jobs, traffic, education, social services, and recreation)
- existing ecosystems, such as wetlands, forests, and desert areas (taking into consideration that the city might have to provide new housing, shopping areas, schools, workplaces, and industry).

There is little argument that human activity has dramatically altered the environment. Opinions differ, however, about what to do about it. In this activity, you will choose to represent a point of view on several complex environmental issues. You will justify your point of view as persuasively as you can.

For each opinion below, decide whether you agree or disagree. (Choose one or the other, even if you are unsure.) Write "AGREE" or "DISAGREE." Then write a paragraph making the case for your decision. Make the case as persuasive as possible.

- Farmland should not be taken for housing, shopping centers, or other urban uses.
- Logging should continue in old growth forests of the northwestern United States. Concern for lost jobs should come before concern for the spotted owl, an animal that logging endangers.
- Any new construction or other project that threatens the quality of America's drinking water should not be allowed.
- People should not be allowed to drive cars on trips of less than one mile in areas with public transportation.
- People who want a lot of children should not worry about the effect of the increasing human population on ecosystems.

Find someone in the class who chose to "agree" with a statement that you chose to "disagree" with or vice versa. Take turns listening carefully to each other's point of view and the reasons for it.

What was the most valid argument that the other person presented? Did the discussion cause you to reconsider your views in any way?

Case Study

Back from the Edge: Recovery of the Red Wolf

The sight of humans made the pair of red wolves nervous. The male, known as #219, paced back and forth in the chain-link pen. The female, known as #330, defensively watched her five pups. Humans visited the pen every day to feed the wolves. But the humans who came to the pen on the afternoon of November 12, 1991, had a different purpose in mind. At 3 P.M., two young women opened the gate and then walked away. The only person left was a cameraman perched in a tree near the pen.

Never before had a camera recorded the release of red wolves into the wild. Both #219 and #330 had been born and bred in captivity. For much of 1991, their entire territory consisted of a 50' x 50' pen in the Cades Cove area of the Great Smoky Mountains National Park. Suddenly, they had miles of woodlands to scent, hunt, and explore.

It took 15 minutes for #219 to edge his way into freedom. His mate moved more cautiously. She sniffed nearly every part of the gate before walking through it. When her pups tried to dart out, #330 drove them back into the pen. The pen would serve as a den and a base site until the family marked a new territory. They were the first red wolves to roam freely in Tennessee for nearly a century. Commented one biologist:

> These first wolves are kind of like astronauts. We're going to let them out and see how they do. . . in the woods.

As the 1970s opened, barely 100 red wolves remained alive. Concerned biologists for the U.S. Fish and Wildlife Department swung into action. Armed with the Endangered Species Act of 1973, they took steps to pull the red wolf back from the edge of extinction.

The Endangered Species Act requires a recovery team for each plant and animal species protected by the law. These teams must organize and regularly update plans to recover a

species so that it can be taken off the endangered list. The plan outlined for the red wolf called for a target population of 550 animals—220 in the wild and 330 in captivity.

Between 1989 and 1993, a total of 301 pups have been born in captivity. Nearly 65-75 percent of these pups have survived.

Release of red wolves forms an important part of the Recovery/Species Plan. The plan calls for three distinct mainland populations of red wolves. Yet, release of a predator is filled with emotion, both pro and con. In 1983, the U.S. Fish and Wildlife Service selected a site known as "Land Between the Lakes," a federally protected area between Kentucky and Tennessee. When news of the project leaked out, a wave of public protest erupted. Hunters, farmers, and livestock owners joined together to block the plan. In early 1984, the Service withdrew its proposal. A headline in a Tennessee newspaper declared: "LBL Plan Killed!"

A hard-taught lesson came from the defeat. Members of the red wolf recovery team learned the importance of public education to the program's success. Commented one biologist: "In our information-driven society, public relations paves the way for science."

In the spring of 1984, the service received a donation of 120,000 acres on a swampy peninsula in North Carolina. A number of factors recommended the land for use in the red wolf project. First, it lay in a thinly populated part of the state. Second, no livestock existed in the area.

To avoid defeat of what became known as the Alligator River National Wildlife Reserve, members of the recovery team kept local officials advised of their plan. They also met with private citizens, including school teachers. Finally, in November 1986, the Point Defiance Zoo shipped four pairs of adult red wolves to Alligator River.

For almost a year, biologists kept the wolves in pens while they adjusted to new smells, sounds, and weather. On September 14, 1987, the recovery team released the first pair. A month later, they released the next three pairs.

Each animal wore a radio collar so that biologists could track them. The notes taken by the biologists opened the door to the world of the red wolf—a world that had nearly been lost a decade before. Field crews studied the range, habits, and food of the red wolf. Even more important, they celebrated the birth of the first red-wolf pups born in the wild.

Between 1987 to 1990, field crews had released 37 redwolves on the reserve. Because each red wolf family needs a 10-50 square-mile territory to hunt, they now asked: "Where do we go from here?" The answer to this question led them to Cades Cove in the Smokies.

The red-wolf pair known as #219 and #330 made history when they walked out of their pen in November 1991. Their tracks marked the return of the red wolf to the southern Appalachians. Other red wolves followed. By August 1993, 13 red wolves lived in Cades Cove, including 6 pups born in the wild.

Through the use of radio collars, field crews have intensely followed the trail blazed by the red wolves of the Smokies. Wolf families showed a dominance over the coyotes. For the most part, they also stayed away from humans. Instead of livestock, the wolves preyed on wild mammals such as raccoons, rabbits, and deer. They also killed at least one wild hog, a major nuisance to farmers in the area.

In late 1993, Gary Henry, Red Wolf Coordinator for the Fish and Wildlife Service, assessed the imporance of the Cades Coves project. Said Henry:

"It's very important that we restore earth's ecosystems. We can't talk about restoring the ecosystem of the Eastern United States without talking about the wolf. At one time it was the top predator of that system. It played an important role in preserving the health of that system."

When Henry spoke these words, the total red-wolf population had grown to 255-260. Of this number, about 198 lived in captivity. The program has stopped the slide of the red wolf into extinction. But the continual survival of the species still rests upon human management.

5 WILDLIFE POPULATIONS

This black howler monkey lives near human communities. Its future depends upon how well people in towns and cities tolerate the wild animals near them.

5.1 People Crowd Out Wildlife

The scientists you read about in the case study are working hard to save the red-wolf population. People who live in North Carolina and Tennessee are also cooperating by not disturbing or killing the wolves that have been released. If it were not for the actions of these people, the red wolves would have no future in the wild. Does this surprise you? You might think that wild **predators**, such as wolves, simply have no need for people.

Why can't wild animals survive on their own?

SURROUNDED BY HUMANS

There are just too many people in the ecosystems that the red wolves used to live in. Cities from Atlanta, Georgia, to Houston, Texas, have grown up into large metropolitan areas. Suburbs spread out from these cities into areas that used to be farms. Wildlife used to have vast areas of nature. But now people live and work in most of those areas. Today, many animal and plant populations are surrounded by human communities and farms. Still other wildlife populations live among people, in the cities and towns.

Some animals can get along fine living close to people. But others, such as the red wolves, cannot. They need large territories in which to hunt. If red wolves have a future, it will be because people decide to take care of their population. Red wolves are the sort of animal that could very easily become extinct.

Not all animal populations are affected in the same way by the activities of people. Certain kinds of animals and plants are more likely than others to vanish from ecosystems. The reason may be that they have characteristics that are not suited to ecosystems taken over by people. Here are the characteristics that make wildlife populations dwindle.

Low population density

Some kinds of animals need lots of room to roam and live mostly alone. Some kinds of plants grow only with individuals spread far apart, not clustered together. They have a naturally low population density. Examples are bears, eagles, and the red wolves in the case study.

When people change an ecosystem by living and working in it, they force many of these wildlife populations out of their homes. Many animal and plant populations become broken into fragments, separated by human communities. Animals with low population density then have a difficult time finding one another for mating. This factor

can result in a lower birth rate for the population.

The red wolves in the case study were released in a large area with no permanent human residents. One reason is that just one wolf pack needs an area measuring hundreds of square kilometers in order to survive generation after generation.

Low birth rate

Some populations have a naturally low birth rate. If human actions cause the populations' death rate to rise, the population will decrease and may even become extinct.

Elephants and rhinoceroses in Africa are good examples. A female elephant may give birth to one offspring only once every four or five years. These animals can't adjust their birth rates to make up for high death rates. In Africa today, elephants and rhinos have high death rates caused by people killing them.

The California condor in the United States is another example of an endangered species with a naturally low birth rate. A mated pair of condors usually can raise one chick about every three years in the wild.

Food specialists

In Chapter 1, you read about the endangered black-footed ferret. This animal specializes in killing and eating ground squirrels known as prairie dogs. But when many of the prairie-dog populations were wiped out by ranchers and farmers, the ferret lost its food supply. The ferret population then became nearly extinct.

Limited range

The range of a population describes how much geographic area it can occupy. Some wildlife populations occur across an entire continent—or an ocean. These populations have a vast range. But other kinds of wildlife depend on a

Penguin populations may vanish if their nesting and feeding habitats are used by people.

small area for their survival. The penguins shown in the photograph on this page, for example, swim across vast stretches of ocean to feed. They nest, however, on only a few islands. If humans damaged or destroyed these island ecosystems, most of the penguins would be unable to reproduce. This would cause a rapid population crash.

All of the factors described above are reasons why there are so many wildlife populations in danger of dying out.

How do human activities endanger wildlife?

ENCROACHING ON WILDLIFE

Whenever a wild land is lost to human use, wildlife is affected. Plants disappear and animals can no longer meet their basic needs for food, water,

and shelter. The animals must either migrate to another location or die.

When humans pollute the air, water, or soil with chemical waste, they threaten many more species of wildlife than hunting, trapping, and fishing put together. The direct and indirect effects of human activity have endangered 2,300 species of animals and 24,000 kinds of plants.

Some people endanger wildlife directly when they take wild plants and animals to sell. Others endanger wildlife by killing animals that are interfering with their business activities in some way. These practices reduce some wildlife populations faster than the populations can replace themselves.

Many people of the world get their food from plants, fish, poultry, and livestock that are raised for food. In developing countries, however, many people still fish, hunt, and trap wild animals and pick wild plants for food. Wild animals, such as monkeys, turtles, lizards, and hummingbirds, are not commonly eaten in industrialized countries. They are, however, eaten as sources of protein in other lands. In fact, in at least 62 countries, 20 percent or more of the animal protein in people's diets comes from wildlife and fish.

Fish provide high-quality protein for people in many parts of the world. As the human population grows, the numbers of fish being caught to feed humans increases. The oceans can produce approximately 100 million tons of fish each year. Yet, overfishing seems to be significantly reducing some fish populations. The United Nations monitors 280 types of fish. It considers 42 types depleted and another 25 slightly to moderately overused.

Commercial hunting or trapping animals for products other than food also endangers animals. In a typical year, 50,000 live primates, 4 million live birds, 10 million reptile skins, 15 million furs, about 350 million tropical fish, ivory from the tusks of 70,000 African elephants, and 1 million orchids are found in markets around the world.

Several species of whales have become endangered because of the demand for whale oil. Some spotted cats, such as the cheetah, have been killed in large numbers for their fur. So have some other animals, such as the otter.

Some kinds of lizards, snakes, and crocodiles are heavily hunted for their skins. Sea turtles are hunted for food and for their shells. Wildflowers are taken and sold to people who want exotic flowers in their greenhouses. Wild animals are taken and sold as pets. Today, local laws or international agreements protect many species. Unfortunately, the protection has come after they are already endangered.

Sometimes, people hunt and trap wild animals because they interfere with agricultural activities that make money. For example, ranchers have killed large numbers of wolves in parts of the United States. The wolves were raiding sheep and cattle herds for food. The wolf is now protected, but not everyone agrees that it should be.

The extinctions of species should not be taken lightly. In nature, everything is so interdependent that to affect one species is to affect many. It has been estimated that whenever one species becomes extinct, about ten more become threatened. Scientists are concerned because the pace of extinction seems to be increasing.

Wildlife populations need to be protected while they are still abundant. When people wait until a population is practically extinct, it may be too late to keep the population in the wild. For the red wolf, it was almost too late. Fortunately, biologists have been successful in releasing animals into the wild in two different parts of North Carolina. Unfortunately, there will probably never be one continuous population across the entire state. There are simply too many people living in between the two reintroduced groups.

You Solve It

Suppose there is a population of 50 red wolves in a national park. The biologists in charge of the population decide that the park has a carrying capacity of 100 wolves. If the wolves double their population in 10 years, what is their annual percent rate of growth?

If the population of 50 wolves increases at about the same rate as the human population of the world—about 1.8 percent per year—how many years will be needed to double the wolf population?

SECTION REVIEW

1. About how many years would it take for a mated pair of California condors to breed enough offspring to replace themselves in the population?

2. Can you think of any wild animals in your community that have very specialized food needs? Could one small change in the environment wipe out the food supply for this animal's population?

3. What is the difference between the number of endangered plant populations and the number of endangered animal populations? Why do you think this difference exists?

FOR DISCUSSION

If any of the red wolves released in North Carolina kill a farmer's domestic cow or other livestock, what should be done? Should the farmer be paid the market value of the animal? Should the wolves be shot or be trapped and put back in captivity?

Refuges can protect many wildlife populations, yet are seldom large enough for animals that need vast areas, such as these bison.

5.2 People Conserve Wildlife

What can people do to conserve wildlife populations?

Endangered wildlife populations do make a comeback sometimes. One example is the American alligator. This animal was once on the U.S. endangered-species list, mainly due to overhunting. After the hunting was halted, the alligator population increased rapidly. Alligator populations can have a high birth rate and inhabit a large geographic range. They are not specialized in their food habits. So they are not limited by the factors described earlier in this chapter. With very little help from people, the American alligator population has rebounded.

This example, however, is unusual. Most wildlife conservation is difficult, and requires work by lots of people.

RESTORING POPULATIONS

Here are a few of the ways that people conserve wildlife populations:
- creation of refuges for plants and animals in habitats where their populations are still abundant;
- improving habitat so that it can support more wildlife;
- relocation, that is, moving organisms from one location to another in order to start up a new population;
- breeding organisms in captivity, then releasing them in the wild.

Refuges People can set aside special places known as wildlife refuges. Refuges can provide wildlife populations with most of their survival needs, if they are located carefully. Refuges are not always complete ecosystems. They may, therefore, require special care by people.

Protecting a population just by providing a refuge does not prevent problems. Wildlife does not recognize the boundaries of refuges. Animals and plants have a natural tendency to disperse.

In Yellowstone National Park, in Wyoming, bison, elk, and brown bears have part of a vast ecosystem to help them survive. But these animals also wander outside the borders of the national park into areas where farmers and ranchers are trying to raise crops and domestic animals. Ranchers don't really want to share the grazing land with wild herds of bison. Bison might spread disease to herds of cattle.

Brown bears are also protected in Yellowstone National Park. But the bears roam outside the park as well.

The park alone is not large enough to contain the entire population of brown bears in the ecosystem. Because brown bears are capable of killing domestic animals, such as cattle, ranchers can shoot a bear that is near their herds.

Wildlife refuges will never be big enough to protect all animal and plant populations. Some wild populations will need to be tolerated in and around farms, cities, and towns. If people can learn to live alongside wildlife without conflict, more plant and animal populations will survive in the future.

Some wildlife populations cause damage to humans. Farmers need to be compensated when wildlife ruins their crops. African elephants, for example, live in protected refuges and parks in several African nations. Elephants, like the bears and bison of Yellowstone, don't recognize borders

People have created new habitats for marine populations by starting artificial reefs near the shore.

drawn by people on a map. They often roam into farmlands, destroying crops that families depend upon. Several African governments have policies to pay farmers for damage to their crops caused by elephants.

Habitat improvement   Scientists and conservationists are now experimenting with different ways of changing land and water habitats. The purpose is to improve conditions for certain wildlife populations. One example is the creation of artificial reefs in coastal ocean waters. To make an artificial reef, people sink old ships or even old motor vehicles in the ocean near the shore. These structures become a habitat for invertebrates such as shellfish. This in turn attracts both small and large fish, which can use the area around the reef as a breeding ground.

Relocation   Plant and animal populations often vanish from habitats where they once thrived. People can aid such wildlife populations by moving some organisms from one location where they still live to a second location. The idea is to conserve a species by starting new populations in several places. The relocation sites are often selected in habitats where a population of an endangered species used to live.

Conservationists now use this method in many parts of the world. It has been tried with all sorts of wildlife, from rare prairie plants in Illinois, to large rhinoceroses in African nations such as Zimbabwe. One recent example is in Belize, a small nation next to Mexico.

Black howler monkeys used to live in most of that nation's forests. They have been gradually pushed into smaller and smaller areas. A team of biologists from several conservation organizations in Belize and the United States cooperated in relocating howler monkeys. They trapped some individuals from one population and then moved them to a distant site where this species used to live.

Captive breeding and release The release of red wolves in North Carolina was made possible because zoos in the United States bred them and built up a captive population. At present, these zoos have room for about 200 red wolves. The captive population cannot be increased unless more space for red wolves is made available.

You Solve It

You are a biologist who manages a wildlife refuge for a private nature-conservation organization. Imagine that the refuge shelters endangered species of trees, wildflowers, and animals, such as the red wolf. Scientists tell you that there is a good possibility that there is an oil and natural gas deposit beneath the land and waters of your refuge.

Should you permit drilling for oil and gas? Make a list of the problems and benefits of doing so. Based on your list, decide your course of action. Write up a plan for protecting your refuge.

SECTION REVIEW

1. In Kenya, an African nation, the government's wildlife agency has suggested putting fences around the wildlife refuges. Make a list of what you think are the advantages and disadvantages of doing so.

2. How would you answer a person who claims that making artificial reefs is nothing more than dumping litter on the ocean floor?

FOR DISCUSSION

What should be done with bison that roam beyond the boundaries of a national park or refuge into private land?

"As human population increases, we're pushing animals into more and more confined spaces," said Heather Eager. Heather is a student zoo curator at the Trevor Zoo, which is operated by her high school, the Millbrook School in Millbrook, New York.

Heather and about 40 other students work in the zoo. There are nearly 150 animals in the zoo, which includes 16 kinds of mammals, 18 kinds of birds, plus reptiles and fish. There are seven endangered species in the zoo, including a group of red wolves. Each animal enclosure has a student keeper who must make sure that the animals' quarters are clean every day.

Why does Heather's high school have a zoo? The school curriculum connects each zoo exhibit to an environmental problem, such as destruction of habitats. The zoo director, Jonathan Meigs, claims that the teachers use the zoo in their courses, including subjects such as art and literature. The school offers three science electives that use the zoo extensively. These courses are ecology, animal behavior, and the role of the modern zoo. "Students respond favorably to working with live animals," Meigs said.

Beyond the courses, the students working in the zoo have important responsibilities. When the zoo's pair of red wolves gave birth to a litter of pups, for example, the students became involved in the care of the newborns. The health of each pup had to be watched carefully. To prevent bacterial infections in the young wolves, the students treated them with antibiotic ointment and oral drops.

Many of the students in the zoo program think that these work-related responsibilities are their most important learning experiences. As Nathaniel Thompson, a senior, explained, "You pick up knowledge doing day-to-day chores." Heather added that her zoo responsibilities made her "a lot more conscious of other environmental issues, such as pollution and recycling."

Heather and other students are concerned about what humans can do to conserve wildlife populations. She's worried that as humans need more room on the earth, there will be less space for wild animals. What message do the students have for others of their generation? Nathaniel summed it up: "We have to try and undo environmental problems . . . through education."

Glossary

abiotic   nonliving parts of the environment that include chemicals in the air, water, and soil, 15

acid rain   rain with a level of acidity that is greater than normal due to air pollution, 65

biomass fuels   living materials, such as trees and grass, that are used as fuels, 65

biotic   pertaining to living things, 15

birth rate   the number of births per 1000 persons in a population in a given year, 10

carrying capacity   the maximum number of organisms that an ecosystem can support, 14

census   an official, usually periodic, count of population and recording of economic status, age, sex, etc., 6

death rate   the number of deaths per 1000 persons in a population in a given year, 10

deforestation   the removal or trees and other vegetation on a large scale, 59

demographers   people that study the human population size, growth, density, and age distribution, 26

demographic transition   the pattern of population growth exhibited by many industrialized countries; as the standard of living increases, both birth and death rates decline, 21

density   numbers of individuals per unit of area, 7

environmental refugees   people who leave their homes or country due to a polluted or unproductive environment, 38

emigration   the departure of individuals from a population in a specific area or country, 11

estimation   a judgment or general calculation of size, amount, or quantity, 6

extinct   no longer in existence, 6

fertility rate   average number of offspring born to females in a population, 29

greenhouse gases   atmospheric gases or vapors that absorb outgoing heat energy emitted from the earth, 65

immigration   the movement of individuals into an area or country, 11

infant mortality   number of infants under 1 year of age dying per 1000 births in any given year, 29

irrigation   the process of supplying land with water by means of artificial ditches, channels, and by sprinklers, 64

life expectancy   the number of years that an individual of a given age may expect on the average to live, 21

limiting factors   the dominant factors that restrict the continued reproduction or spread of a particular species, 15

metropolitan area   a population area consisting of a central city and smaller surrounding communities, 42

nonrenewable resources natural resources such as coal or mineral ores that are not replaceable after their removal, 54

overgrazing too much plant-eating by grazing animals, such as cattle, so that the plant populations are severely reduced, 59

population all members of a single species living in a certain area at the same time, 5

population age structure a description of the ages of members of a population that shows the number of individuals in each age class, 27

predators animals that capture and eat other animals, 72

random distribution spatial location of individuals purely by chance, 17

refugees people who leave their homes or country to live in another, as in a time of war, 38

renewable resources resources that can be used continuously without being used up, 54

subsistence agriculture raising plants or animals in order to meet the basic food needs of the family, 56

uniform distribution spatial location of individuals such that the distance between individuals is roughly equal throughout the population, 17

Resource Directory

HUMAN POPULATION ORGANIZATIONS

Center for Communication Programs
Johns Hopkins University
527 St. Paul Place
Baltimore, MD 21202
   Supports public awareness of family planning; maintains the Population Information Program, the world's largest computerized bibliography on human populations.

Center for Development and Population Activities
1717 Massachusetts Ave., NW
Washington, DC 20036
   Trains and supports individuals from developing countries on the management of their human population; maintains a library of more than 500 books, as well as pamphlets, newsletters, and other references on population and national development.

Population Association of America
1722 N St., NW
Washington, DC 20036
   Studies the social and scientific aspects of changes in human populations; publishes Demography, *a journal issued four times a year.*

Population Communication
1489 East Colorado Blvd.
Pasadena, CA 91106
   Supports the control of global population by making population information available to people in developing countries.

Population Council
1 Dag Hammarskjold Plaza
New York, NY 10017
   Publishes information on population issues in developing countries, such as contraceptive development, family planning, women's roles, and the health of pregnant women and newborns.

Population-Environment Balance
1325 G St., NW
Washington, DC 20005
   Sponsors educational programs and media campaigns to make Americans aware of the negative effects of population growth on the environment.

Population Institute
110 Maryland Ave., NE
Washington, DC 20002
   Composed of doctors, lawyers, religious leaders, educators, and other concerned people who sponsor educational and political programs to control global overpopulation.

Population Reference Bureau
1875 Connecticut Ave., NW
Washington, DC 20009
   Compiles information on population trends in the United States and throughout the world; provides population materials through catalog sales; publishes the Population Handbook: A Quick Guide to Population Dynamics for Journalists, Policymakers, Teachers, Students, and Other People Interested in People.

Population Renewal Office
36 West 59th St.
Kansas City, MO 64113
   Advocates population growth rather than population control; supplies research findings to writers, journalists, teachers, and students.

Society for the Study of Social Biology
East-West Population Institute
1777 East-West Rd.
Honolulu, HI 96848
   Studies the connection between heredity and population; seeks to find the social, cultural, and biological forces that affect the growth of human populations.

World Population Society
1333 H St., NW
Washington, DC 20005
   Distributes educational materials on population change and its effect on human needs.

Zero Population Growth
1400 16th St., NW
Washington, DC 20036
 Provides educational programs and publications concerning global population growth to teachers and students.

WILDLIFE POPULATION ORGANIZATIONS

African Wildlife Foundation
1717 Massachusetts Ave., N.W.
Washington, DC 20036
 Operates wildlife conservation projects in Africa; carries out conservation education programs for schools.

Atlantic Salmon Federation
PO Box 429
St. Andrews, NB, Canada EOG 2XO
 Promotes the preservation and management of Atlantic salmon; sponsors research and educational projects.

Bat Conservation International
PO Box 162603
Austin, TX 78716
 Seeks to increase public awareness of the ecological value of bats; promotes conservation and management of bat populations.

Billfish Foundation
2051 NW 11th St.
Miami, FL 33125
 Promotes the conservation of billfish through scientific research and educational programs.

Caribbean Conservation Corporation
P. O. Box 2866
Gainesville, FL 32602
 Conducts conservation programs for marine turtles throughout the world.

Center for Marine Conservation
1725 DeSales St., N.W.
Suite 500
Washington, DC 20036
 Provides education and public information regarding conservation of fish and other marine wildlife.

Center for Plant Conservation
P. O. Box 299
St. Louis, MO 63166
 Dedicated to the conservation of rare plants.

Cornell Laboratory of Ornithology
159 Sapsucker Woods Road
Ithaca, NY 14850
 Promotes conservation of bird populations.

Defenders of Wildlife
1244 19th St., NW
Washington, DC 20036
 Promotes the preservation and protection of wildlife through education and research; maintains a speaker's bureau and sponsors wildlife education programs.

Endangered Species Coalition
1050 Thomas Jefferson St., NW
Washington, DC 20007
202 333 7481
 Supports the protection of endangered and threatened animals and plants by encouraging international cooperation.

Global Tomorrow Coalition
1325 G Street, N.W.
Suite 1010
Washington, DC 20005
 Promotes understanding of global trends in population, resources, and environment.

Great Bear Foundation
PO Box 2699
Missoula, MT 59806
406 721 3009
 Dedicated to the protection of bears and their habitat; provides educational books and materials for people who live near bears.

International Crane Foundation
E-11376 Shady Lane Rd.
Baraboo , WI 53913
608 356 9462

Committed to the preservation of the crane and its natural habitat; maintains a speakers, bureau and sponsors educational programs.

Jane Goodall Institute For Wildlife Research, Education, And Conservation

PO Box 41720
Tucson, AZ 85717
602 325 1211
Conducts field research and sponsors educational programs on chimpanzees.

Manomet Bird Observatory

PO Box 1770
Manomet, MA 02345
508 224 6521
Publishes census records of migratory land birds, shore birds, and sea birds.

Mountain Lion Foundation

PO Box 1896
Sacramento, CA 95812
916 442 2666
Dedicated to the preservation and long-term survival of the cougar and its habitat; conducts field research and sponsors educational programs.

National Geographic Society

1145 17th St., NW
Washington, DC 20036
Publishes articles on wildlife in National Geographic Magazine *and offers videotapes on wildlife that include:*
African Wildlife (1981); *Gorilla* (1981); *Among the Wild Chimpanzees* (1984); *Land of the Tiger* (1985); *Grizzlies* (1987); *Antarctic Wildlife Adventure* (1991); and *Killer Whales* (1993).

National Institute for Urban Wildlife

10921 Trotting Ridge Way
Columbia, MD 21044
Provides information about urban wildlife populations.

National Wildlife Federation

8925 Leesburg Pike
Vienna, VA 22184

Supports the wise use and proper management of wildlife; publishes International Wildlife *on a monthly basis.*

Pacific Whale Foundation

Kealia Beach Plaza
101 North Kihei Rd.
Kihei, HI 96753
808 879 8811
Dedicated to the protection of marine mammals; publishes material on marine mammals and their habitat.

Raptor Education Foundation

21901 East Hampden Ave.
Aurora, CO 80013
303 680 8500
Sponsors educational programs about raptors to ensure their preservation; provides lectures with live raptors for classrooms, as well as for youth and senior groups.

Save The Manatee Club

500 North Maitland Ave.
Maitland, FL 32751
407 539 0990
Dedicated to help save the West Indian manatee and its habitat; conducts workshops and sponsors educational outreach programs for schools and environmental clubs.

The Wildlife Conservation Society

2300 Southern Boulevard
Bronx, NY 10460
Provides educational programs for schools; publishes Wildlife Conservation *magazine.*

Wolf Haven International

3111 Offut Lake Rd.
Tenino, WA 98589
206 264 4695
Seeks to educate the public and increase awareness of the need for conservation of wolves; sponsors educational programs presented in schools and other educational institutions.

Index

environmental refugees, 38-39
Monkey, howler monkeys, 79

N

Natural disasters, effects on population, 39
Natural resources
    consumption and wealth, 54
    nonrenewable resources, 54
    renewable resources, 54
Nomads, life of, 2-4
Nonrenewable resources, nature of, 54

O

Oceania, population of, 32
Overcrowding, 16, 37
Overfishing, 75
Overgrazing, grasslands, 59-60

P

Penguins, 74
Population
    birth rate, 10
    carrying capacity, 14-15
    death rate, 10
    definition of, 5
    density, 7
    distribution of, 17-18
    and emigration, 11
    growth rate, measurement of, 10-11
    and immigration, 11
    limiting factors, 15-17
    measurement of, 6-7
    overcrowding, 16
    size of, 6
    See also Human population growth
Population age structure, 27-28
Population Communications
    International (PCI), 43
Population control
    international population agencies,
    43, 44
    See also Family planning
Population crash, 14

Population pressures, 37-39
Potato famine, 11
Predators, 15, 72
Profamilia, 50

R

Random distribution, 17
Reefs, artificial, 78-79
Refuges, wildlife conservation, 77-79
Renewable resources, nature of, 54
Replacement-level fertility, 29
Reptiles, commercial hunting, 75
Rhinoceros, 73
Rule of 70, 26

S

Somalia, 18
Southeast Asia, population growth, 30
Subsistence agriculture, 56
Suburbs, 37

T

Tibet, Drokbas of, 2-4
Total fertility rates, 29
Tropical forests, destruction of, 59

U

Uniform distribution, 17
United States
    family planning, 52
    population growth, 27, 31
    suburban dwellers, 37
Urban areas. See Cities

W

Wan-xi-shao, 51
Water shortages, 66-67
Wetlands
    ecosystems of, 61-62
    filling of, 61-62

Photo Acknowledgments

1: Reuters/Bettmann;   **3:** © Art Wolfe;   **4:** Dr. Melvin Goldstein;
5: Dr. Melvin Goldstein;   **15:** © Tim Clark;   **16:** Michael Giannechini/Photo
Researchers;   **23:** Reuters/Bettmann;   **42:** © Edward Slater/The Stock Shop;
44: Courtesy of Media/Materials Collection at the Johns Hopkins Center of
Communication;   **45:** George H. Harrison/Grant Heilman;   **51:** Courtesy of
Media/Materials Collection at the Johns Hopkins Center for Communication;
54: Grant Heilman;   **56:** United Nations;   **58:** Reuters/Bettmann;   **60:** United
Nations;   **61:** Grant Heilman;   **64:** Grant Heilman;   **66:** UPI/Bettmann;
67: United Nations;   **69:** © Art Wolfe;   **71:** Courtesy of Roland Smith/The Red
Wolf Newsletter;   **72:** © Art Wolfe;   **74:** © Gregory J. Dimijian/Photo
Researchers;   **77:** © Art Wolfe;   **78:** © John Holden Bailey/Tom Stack and
Associates;   **81:** © Sven Martson, New Haven, CT.